A CATHEDRAL OF MUSIC

THE ARCHIVIO STORICO RICORDI

ARCHIVIO STORICO RICORDI

BERTELSMANN

PRESTEL
München · London · New York

Editorial

Dear Readers,

for an international media company like Bertelsmann, the ideas and creativity of our artists, writers and journalists form the heart of our value creation. They are the ones who constantly reinvent what we have to offer — and tell stories that provide information, entertainment and inspiration day after day. I am therefore delighted that, in this book about the Archivio Storico Ricordi, we have the privilege of telling a story that has not only inspired many music lovers over the past 200 years, but that is also about the preservation of an important piece of European cultural heritage.

The Archivio bears witness to the achievements of a company whose name still stands as a symbol of the connection between art and society. The use of the archive and the communication of its contents to the outside preserve and activate a legacy whose cultural-historical relevance is steadily growing. Its importance for research and education cannot be overstated.

The Ricordi archive has been part of Bertelsmann since 1994. When we sold the associated parent company in 2006, we deliberately decided to keep the archive — to preserve its valuable collection of music history for posterity, and to give it greater visibility. The extraordinary scope of the collection and its outstanding importance for the history of Italian opera were reason enough to secure the almost 8 000 scores, 10 000 librettos, 15 000 letters and many other documents and to present them in a new form.

On behalf of Bertelsmann, I am delighted that we can tell the story of Ricordi and the archive's collections in detail in this publication. In this spirit, I am very pleased about your interest in Archivio Storico Ricordi and wish you an enjoyable read!

Kind regards,

Thomas Rabe
Chairman & CEO of Bertelsmann

Preface

"The Archivio Ricordi is a cathedral of music, unique in the world."

LUCIANO BERIO

In the heart of Milan's Brera district, in the Biblioteca Braidense, a mere ten-minute walk from the Scala, is the most important private music archive in Italy: the Archivio Storico Ricordi.

The origins of the archive date back to 1808 when the copyist and violinist Giovanni Ricordi founded his music publishing company basing his work initially on his contracts with various Milanese theaters, which secured him ownership of the parts and reductions he produced. This was the beginning of the collection, which grew steadily after the founding of the Ricordi publishing house and now contains a wealth of research material and information. The material relates to areas as diverse as the history of the Ricordi publishing house itself and of music publishing, theater history, social history, the history of European music — with an emphasis on musical theater —, the history of stage and costume design, as well as that of fashion and graphic reproduction of the late 19th century through to the 1920s and 1930s.

So right in the middle of the city where opera history was written in the 19th century, you can immerse yourself in a world that comes vividly alive through autographs, libretto manuscripts, letters, original set and costume designs.

The archive is unique for several reasons. The wealth of documents alone is impressive. It consists of around 8 000 manuscript scores, over 10 000 librettos from the 17th to the 20th century, approximately 15 000 letters from composers and librettists, over 10 000 stage designs and figurines (stage costumes painted on dolls), over 6 000 photographs, posters, drawings and prints. With its diverse inventory, the archive provides unparalleled information about the history and aesthetics of opera in the 19th and 20th centuries — the "golden age" of Italian opera in the 19th century, from about 1830 to 1910, the time of change in the first decade of the 20th century and the following decades until 1945, and the post-war period with its significant innovations to the opera genre in Italy. The archive also tells the history of Italy's foremost music publishing company, which had an international impact and also was formative in the general history of music.

Originally established as a business archive, the Archivio Storico Ricordi documents and illustrates the changes that the Ricordi publishing house, which existed as an independent company until 1994, underwent, as well as developments in the national and international music business in the context of European history. For one important part of the archive is the publisher's business correspondence, which is complete until about the middle of the 20th century. This as yet largely unexplored collection of the surviving "copialettere" — copies of all outgoing mail from 1888 to 1962 — is a treasure trove and starting point for many fields of research into the history of music, but also the history of the company and the industry, as well as political and social history.

Finally, Archivio Storico Ricordi is a "lieu de mémoire", a place of memory for Italian and European cultural history. Opera as an art form, as an Italian creation initially a source of Italian cultural identity, also became a politically charged medium in the 19th century. Starting from the early days of opera in the 17th century, with Jacopo Peri and above all Monteverdi, the impetus of Italian opera is also crucial for the history of music, especially of European music. No opera composer can develop without this tradition, whether they choose to corroborate it or turn away from it. Likewise, every opera visitor today must turn towards or away from this tradition. Performance schedules worldwide are full of works of musical theater once successfully launched by Ricordi as innovations.

Italian opera is a central element in communicating European cultural history in the field of music. The Archivio Storico Ricordi is an illustrative place in educational terms as well: an interactive, multi-media presentation of materials from the archive using digital platforms can turn the world of opera as part of cultural history into a tangible experience for students. The immediacy of historical documents is still of great value, even in a world of media. This is true for research as well: although digitized media do indeed convey the content of the text, they do not provide information about other factors that are important for the classification and evaluation of original historical documents, such as paper and ink, binding, and the like.

So the work of the archive, and working in and with the archive, takes a dual approach. The first is "inward", whereby researchers from relevant disciplines study, evaluate, publish and comment on the documents. And secondly "outward", whereby the materials are prepared for and presented in various media. It almost goes without saying that they give rise to different focuses. Nor are there clear-cut boundaries: research findings can lead to performances, reconstructions and exhibitions that stimulate the interest of the general public. In turn, educational presentations or those meant for the general public can explore media, communications, and economic-social mechanisms that enrich research.

These themes are revealed in three steps:

1
The history of the Ricordi publishing house from 1808 to 1994. It is shaped by personalities who embody and reflect Italian history in particular, but also the history of Europe from the early 19th century until the end of the 20th century.

2
The Archivio Storico Ricordi and its documents. These convey a significant part of world cultural history. Italian opera in the 19th century and its development in the 20th century become immediately tangible. The documents serve to illustrate 19th-century opera, and help in understanding the genre of opera as an aesthetic and cultural-historical phenomenon.

3
An appendix containing an overview of the stored documents in the archive, and an index of names.

In the year 1808, Giovanni Ricordi founds a music publishing company in Milan, which will significantly shape Italian and European cultural history in the 19th and 20th centuries: Casa Ricordi, which will go on to publish the works of Italy's "big five" opera composers: Gioachino Rossini, Gaetano Donizetti, Vincenzo Bellini, Giuseppe Verdi and Giacomo Puccini. But many other musicians find their way to Casa Ricordi, a company that is symbolically synonymous with Italian music.

A BRIEF HISTORY OF THE RICORDI PUBLISHING HOUSE

1

The Hard Worker: Giovanni Ricordi

The period from 1808 to 1853

Giovanni Ricordi (1785–1853), a professional violinist and copyist, starts collecting scores and librettos at an early stage. This collection is the beginning of the Archivio Storico Ricordi. From 1803 Giovanni signs contracts with various Milan theaters – the Teatro Carcano, the Teatro del Lentasio and the Teatro Girolamo – granting him the rights to distribute some of the scores he has produced. The contracts give him the right to sell piano reductions or orchestral parts, for example. This is how the foundations of the archive are created.

It is a time when the music publishing industry in Italy, modeled on that of Germany, France and England, is beginning to flourish. The French Revolution is a good 15 years in the past; Napoleon has launched his campaign in Europe; the Industrial Revolution is spreading from Great Britain to Central and Southern Europe. In Milan especially, the *Restaurazione* of the Napoleonic years makes the city a principal hub of publishing activity in Italy and a pole of attraction for intellectuals in various fields of the arts[1]. The Milan conservatory of music (based on the model of the Paris Conservatoire) is founded in 1808 (the same year as the founding of the Ricordi firm). The time had come, as it were, for a company like Casa Ricordi. This wasn't primarily about the idea of developing a publishing house, but about putting such an idea into practice in conjunction with societal developments. Giovanni Ricordi is an entrepreneurial genius and a courageous man: In the summer of 1807, he travels to Leipzig to learn techniques of music printing from the established German music publisher Breitkopf & Härtel as an intern, and returns to Milan with a German copperplate engraving press. On January 16, 1808, he convinces the engraver and music dealer Felice Festa to join him in founding the Ricordi publishing house.

1808

The company premises are located in Contrada Santa Margherita, near the cathedral, and despite repeated moves Casa Ricordi always remains in this area. The original foundation document bears the date "Milano questo dì Sabbato 16 Gennajo 1808" and the ornate signatures of the two founders. The document speaks about the founding of a music printer ("stamperia di musica"), which will use both engraving technology ("incisione") and printing technology ("impressione").

1—Giovanni Ricordi, portrait by Antonio Bignoli

Festa leaves the company in June of that year, and Giovanni Ricordi continues to run it alone. Incidentally, the first publications are not operas but purely instrumental compositions: *Fantasia con variazioni* by Abate Moro, *Le stagioni dell'anno* by Antonio Nava for "French guitar", and the *Giornale di Musica Vocale Italiana*. This music "magazine" is designed as a subscription publication. Each issue contains 360 pages[2]. Giovanni manages to sign contracts with other Milan theaters, which give him ever more favorable conditions regarding the exploitation of the material he produces. One clever move is Ricordi's commitment to music-teaching materials. In 1812 he publishes a piano tutorial by the pianist and composer Francesco Pollini, and that same year becomes the official publisher for the Milan Conservatory ("Editore del Regio Conservatorio e delle Case di Educazione del Regno").

In 1814 the first catalog is published, a milestone in the short history of the publishing house: *Catalogo della musica stampata nella nuova calcografia di Giovanni Ricordi* with 142 items in addition to 35 items of music from the first three years of the *Giornale di Musica*[3]. It is striking once again that the catalog mainly lists instrumental music. This corresponds to the taste of the times, which is still influenced by that of the 18th century; but above all, it meets the demands for music "in the home" on the part of skilled dilettantes and appassionati in the substantial and growing market of the rising European middle class. The presence of Ricordi's opera composers in the catalog of printed music, as a reflection of the lucrative "rental" business of music materials (for professional and dilettante performing groups), is yet to come. What Giovanni writes for the catalog's users in the preface is also interesting: he addresses the "Signori Dilettanti" (amateur musicians), the "Professori di Musica" (music teachers), and the "Impresarj di Teatro" (theater directors). This heralds the emergence of a bourgeois society in which music played at home is part of everyday life, in which music is taught, in which theater is moving away from the courtly form and is becoming a "business".

From December 1814, Giovanni Ricordi also works as a copyist and prompter at La Scala. His name now appears in the librettos and, from 1820, also on the title page (as "Editore e proprietario della musica" — "publisher and owner of the music.")

2—3

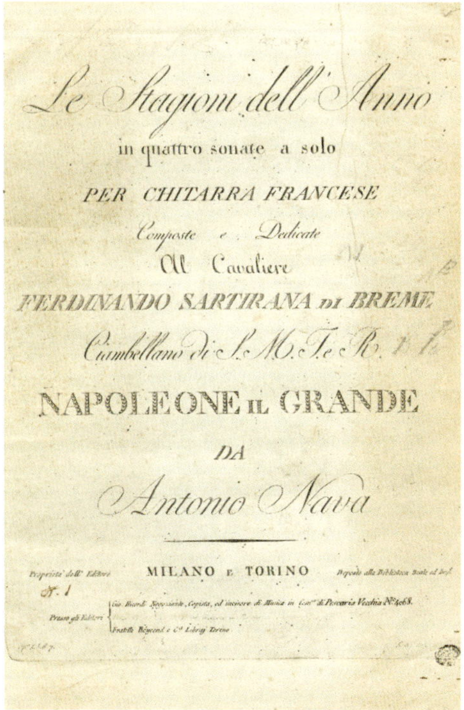

The second Casa Ricordi catalog, which appears in 1815, already shows a trend towards opera. Ricordi has now achieved a certain reputation. He trains apprentices in copper engraving (including Francesco Lucca, who later becomes his great rival as a publisher), and expands his archive.

His main business is rentals of music performing material to theaters. Over the years, the Teatro alla Scala grants him progressively non-restrictive permissions for the exploitation of sheet music material. These soon apply regardless of individual contracts. Ricordi's position in relation to the theaters becomes increasingly stronger, and his archive grows continually. Finally, in 1825, La Scala sells him its entire inventory[4].

1825

He pays 300 Austrian lire for them on the condition that he reduces the rental fees for La Scala. That same year, the *Gran Catalogo* is published with about 2 500 items. It contains the first references to the centrally located Ricordi branch offices in Florence (Via dei Calzajoli) and London (Piccadilly)[5]. Ricordi opens the "Litografia Ricordi"[6], and his son Tito joins the business. Tito is a talented artist and, like his father, has learned the printing trade in Germany. The "Litografia" is important because it points the way to the later elaborate design of the jackets in the Officine Grafiche (typography), which will become a hallmark of the Ricordi publishing house. The Archivio Storico Ricordi possesses a number of artistically beautiful editions. For the history of design, this is an example from the field of music publishing that demonstrates how graphic design developed from the mid-19th to early 20th century.

Around the turn of the century, the Officine also became enormously important in the graphics used for posters and publicity material. The archive also has a large collection in this field.

2—*Le stagioni dell'anno* by Antonio Nava, first printed edition by Casa Ricordi, 1808
3—Giuseppe Verdi, portrait by Roberto Focosi

1844 marks the publication of the first catalog that doesn't advertise the publishing company's production "expressis verbis", but presents it as self-evident.[7] The company has now resided in its prestigious offices at 1720, Contrada degli Omenoni, for six years. It has enough space for all the publishing departments and a sales room. The focus is now clearly on music for the theater — house composers include Rossini, Bellini, Mercadante and Donizetti (the German-Italian composer Simone Mayr had introduced him to Giovanni Ricordi in 1815), and of course Giuseppe Verdi, whose 1842 opera *Nabucco* is a worldwide success and initiates the era of Verdi.

Giuseppe Verdi and Giovanni Ricordi are kindred spirits when it comes to their view of the opera genre as an aesthetic and social phenomenon, and run a joint project for its further development. The meeting of these two men, each very original personalities in their own way, in a politically, economically and socially turbulent time, makes possible an immense success. They combine artistic quality and market orientation with different emphases: "The quality and artistic design, reorganization of the role of music, close coordination of mediation processes, popular success, economic profit, and growth of the company are elements of a common vision thanks to which Ricordi points the way to a new constitutionality of music — modern, romantic and Italian".[8] "Italian" is an important word here, because Ricordi and Verdi are also joined in their vision of a united Italy in view of the Italian unification movement, the Risorgimento. Starting in 1842, the year of the first performance of *Nabucco*, Verdi's works are overlaid with political messages. To this day, people argue about how his work and its effects interacted here.

1842

In the same year, 1842, Giovanni Ricordi also launches Italy's first musicological magazine, the *Gazzetta Musicale di Milano.* This probably is an early instance of his son Tito I's influence: Tito suggested this magazine also as a way of creating a vehicle for Casa Ricordi to publicize the rights to compositions that it had acquired. The establishment of an effective copyright law is an issue that already concerns Giovanni and intensively occupies Tito I and Giulio.

The *Gazzetta* appears from 1842 to 1902 (with a few interruptions). The archive contains copies from all stages of its publication, so the history of the magazine can be followed by examining the various issues.

The *Gazzetta* is a newsletter (that not only covers publishing rights, but also the cultural life of Milan and reviews of performances) and an organ for discussing issues in music aesthetics. The magazine — based on French and German models — is thus the first periodical of its kind in Italy. Edited by the theater journalist Giacinto Battaglia, it is initially published on Sundays, and from 1847 on Wednesdays. Once a month a composition is enclosed with it. At the end of the year, these twelve compositions appear in an anthology, the *Antologia classica musicale,* and subscribers are once even offered a collection of figurines from romantic opera. The "Cinque Giornate di Milano", the Risorgimento revolt in Milan in March 1848, leads to a first interruption of the publication. But it resumes shortly afterwards, initially with a highly politicized title: *Gazzetta Musicale di Milano ed Eco delle notizie politiche* (Musical Gazette and Political news), and from July as a purely musical magazine once again. The turbulent times lead to the publication of the *Gazzetta* being interrupted several more times. In 1853 Tito I takes over as editor himself, followed by Alberto Mazzucato in 1856 and Filippo Filippi in 1858.

1848

The Ricordi publishing house maintains the practice of publishing an in-house music magazine later on: From 1871 to 1878 the *Rivista Minima* is published, initially as an annual gift for *Gazzetta* subscribers; from 1902 to 1905 *Musica e Musicisti;* from 1906 to 1912 the Art Deco-influenced *Ars et Labor;* from 1919 to 1942 *Musica d'Oggi;* and from 1951 to 1957 *Ricordiana.*

Giovanni Ricordi's work triggers a crucial process in the Italian opera business that also extends to the artistic development of opera in terms of a work's autonomy and uniqueness. Ricordi's conscientious efforts to encourage and promote authors and their work on the one hand, and his nose for business on the other, play a crucial role in turning a small publishing house into a successful and influential company over four decades.

4—First issue of the *Gazzetta Musicale di Milano,* first periodical published by Casa Ricordi, 1842

GAZZETTA MUSICALE DI MILANO

N. 1. DOMENICA 2 Gennajo 1842.

Si pubblica ogni domenica. — Nel corso dell' anno si danno ai signori Associati dodici pezzi di scelta musica classica antica e moderna, destinati a comporre un volume in 4.° di centocinquanta pagine circa, il quale in apposito elegante frontespizio figurato si intittolerà ANTOLOGIA CLASSICA MUSICALE.

« La musique, par des inflexions vives, accentuées, et, » pour ainsi dire, parlantes, exprime toutes les pas» sions, peint tous les tableaux, rend tous les objets, » soumet la nature entière à ses savantes imitations, » et porte ainsi jusqu'au coeur de l'homme des sen» timents propres à l'émouvoir. »

J. J. ROUSSEAU.

Il prezzo dell' associazione annua alla *Gazzetta* e all'*Antologia classica musicale* è di Aust. lire 24 anticipate. Pel semestre e pel trimestre in proporzione. L'affrancazione postale della sola *Gazzetta* per l' interno della Monarchia e per l' estero fino a confini è stabilita ad annue lire 4. — La spedizione dei pezzi di musica viene fatta mensilmente e franca di porto ai diversi corrispondenti dello Studio *Ricordi*, nel modo indicato nel Manifesto. — Le associazioni si ricevono in Milano presso l'Ufficio della *Gazzetta* in casa *Ricordi*, contrada degli Omenoni N.° 1720; all' estero presso i principali negozianti di musica e presso gli Uffici postali. — Le lettere, i gruppi, ec. vorranno essere mandati franchi di porto.

INTRODUZIONE.

Delle attuali condizioni delle arti musicali in Italia.

ARTICOLO I.

I' parlo per ver dire.
PETRARCA.

COLORO, e non sono in picciol numero, i quali hanno in uso di giudicar delle cose dalla sola apparenza e non dall'intima sostanza, vivono nella molto bella opinione che l'Italia d'oggidì sia la terra classica della musica, come tale fu essa ripetutamente proclamata ai floridi giorni dei Cimarosa e dei Paesiello, dei Pacchiarotti e dei Marchesi, delle Bulgarelli, delle Banti ec. E per verità, a chi badi menomamente ai clamorosi trionfi onde ad ogni tratto si onorano nei menomi nostri teatri lirici le tante così dette celebrità musicali di che è formicolante questa bellissima penisola; a chi tenga conto delle tante iperboliche elucubrazioni dei nostri giornali sempre traboccanti della gloria immortale onde si incoronano ad ogni poco non so quante centinaja di esimie prime donne, di incomparabili primi tenori, di celeberrimi baritoni e bassi; a chi si fermi un tratto per le strade maggiori non delle sole nostre capitali, ma ed anco de' menomi borghi, e ammiri nelle vetrine degli editori musicali, de' librai, e de' rivendugliuoli di intagli, i ritratti in litografia di non so quante dozzine di dozzine di eccellenze melodrammatiche, melotragiche e melobuffe, altre disegnate in sembianza di muse antiche inghirlandate di fiori, altre di genii mitologici, altre di olimpici eroi colla gran fronte onusta di allori e riposanti su un letto di palme; a chi tenga conto dei nembi di sonetti, canzoni, inni, ditirambi che tanto spesso veggiam piovere dai loggioni a ingombrar l'atmosfera delle nostre platee grandi e piccole; a chi abbia avuta la santa pazienza di gettar lo sguardo su certe rapsodie teatrali biografico-panegiriche più gonfie di superlativi e ridondanti di magniloquie frasi d'ammirazione che nol fossero di care ghiottornie le botteghe de' nostri salsamentari la vigilia delle or passate feste natalizie...; a tutti costoro, noi diciamo, riescir debbe certamente molto difficile il non persuadersi che noi italiani dei correnti anni di grazia viviamo proprio nell' età dell' oro de' fefautti e de' mibemolli! Eppure, che cosa diranno di noi i nostri lettori se, per conto nostro, non punto allucinati dal falso orpello che ne circonda, avremo il coraggio di mettere innanzi una opinione in gran parte contraria e di protestarci persuasi essere anzi oggidì l'arte musicale in Italia in condizione tutt'altro che invidiabile, minacciato di fallimento qualche ramo di essa, ed altro, per cagioni fatali, spinto a volgere alla sua piena decadenza? - Se non che, prima di tutto intendiamoci bene nei termini; chè non avessero per caso a lapidarci coloro, i quali, per un falso sentimentalismo patriottico, amano meglio essere pascolati di assurde adulazioni, anzi che di ardite ma utili verità; nè ci gridino addietro *alla bestemmia* quegli altri cui la superba albagia delle passate memorie che si stenda a velare i torti della presente ignavia è più gradita della voce di chi scuota dal suo sonno involontario il genio italiano e lo ecciti a non lasciare che le altre nazioni lo precorrano sulla strada dei progressi intellettuali e civili. Noi coll' aver detto che l'arte de' suoni è ora nella nostra Italia in istato di scadimento, non abbiamo voluto per ombra accennare che spenta sia o solo in parte scemata tra noi quella gloriosa e potente favilla musicale che accese il petto ai tanti insigni de' quali si vanta l' italiana melopea. Mai no: siamo anzi preparati a sostenere con ampio corredo di ragioni e di prove a fronte di chiunque osasse mai affermare l' opposto, che fra il vivace e immaginoso popolo nostro più che sotto qualunque altro cielo è sovrano il musicale istinto; che la natura, sì generosa de' suoi più eletti doni all'uomo italiano, nol fu mai tanto come dei tesori di che si costituisce il più puro, il più nobile, il più efficace tra i linguaggi dell'affetto; che una tal qual tendenza fisica ad espandere l' anima coi soavi accenti della musica non venne data da Dio con tanta esuberanza come a questa nazione scaldata dal sole che irradiò le fronti de' più sublimi interpreti del bello artistico. L'Italia del tempo presente, altamente lo proclamiamo, sotto questo particolare aspetto non ha nulla ad invidiare alle sue età musicali più trionfanti; ai dì nostri, come a' tempi de' suoi più grandi capiscuola, l'organizzazione italiana è in sovrana guisa inclinata a riuscir prodigiosa di musicali prodotti; le doti primitive o, diremo meglio, i germi di istinto che si richiedono a costituire i grandi cantanti, i grandi attori, i sommi poeti e compositori, voi li vedete largiti a profusione ove solo gettiate uno sguardo alla innumerevole turba di coloro che tra noi si addensano al limitare delle professioni teatrali; i pubblici più colti d'Europa, con tutta la loro vana pretesa di giudici inappellabili in fatto di dottrinarismo estetico e di sapienza musicale, mal reggerebbero al confronto delle nostre più modeste platee, ove avesse a darsi la palma a chi sapesse mostrar meglio di sentir proprio nel fondo dell'anima il prestigio delle creazioni musicali, a chi valesse meglio a palesare di aver sortita dalla natura indole più propria a simpatizzare, per gusto sincero e non affettato, coll'arte e coll'artista. L' italiano, il diciamo con orgoglio, ove lo si voglia supporre isolato da ogni condizione estranea alla sua indole naturale, va primo a tutti i popoli nel genio artistico, va primissimo nel genio musicale. Ma, poichè abbiamo voluto proclamare con tanta insistente pompa questa incontrastabile verità, ci si vorrà forse negare di affermar ad un tempo con pari franchezza che, per molte ragioni finora solo in nube accennate, (e di queste verremo a suo luogo discorrendo per esteso) quelle arti stesse e l'arte de' suoni non meno dell'altre, per le quali ricevemmo dalla natura tanta dovizia di istintive disposizioni, sono al presente nella patria nostra con limitato senno interpretate, coltivate con insufficienza di larghi principii, e con false ed anguste dottrine giudicate (1)? Ad altri l' ufficio di sostenere questa tesi per ciò che più particolarmente riguarda la pittura, la scultura, la poesia ec.; a noi quello di svolgerla nel proposito della musica. —

Abbiamo più sopra gettato un motto delle professioni teatrali. Ebbene: prendiamo le mosse dal dire alcuna cosa di queste. Chi sà additarne un solo popolo d'Europa, nel seno del quale ribolla come tra noi, e ferva più incomposta, e stiam quasi per dire frenetica, la brama di avventurarsi ad occhi chiusi e a capo basso sul burrascoso oceano della scena melodrammatica? Giovinetti inesperti, mal sortiti in altre umili carriere, respinti dal conteggio, dalla mercatura, o forsanco dalle meccaniche officine, se furono dati per disperati d' ogni mezzo di buona riuscita in altri studii, se ne consolano di leggieri col pensare che rimane loro pur sempre un' àncora di speranza, e un raggio di luce splende pur sempre nel buio del loro avvenire; la carriera del canto! Ed eccoli correre difilati a piantarsi a lato al pianoforte del primo maestruzzo che lor colga tra piedi e a farsi provare a gola spalancata il *metallo* della voce! - È deciso il nuovo destino: Tizio ha un eccellente *diapason* di tenore, Sempronio ha un magnifico registro di basso! Detto fatto le lezioni di solfeggio e di vocalizzazione (e sa

(1) Avvertiamo i lettori che parliamo dello stato dell'arte in genere, e che non saremo tardi a dedicare il nostro culto alle gloriose eccezioni per altro in troppo piccolo numero.....

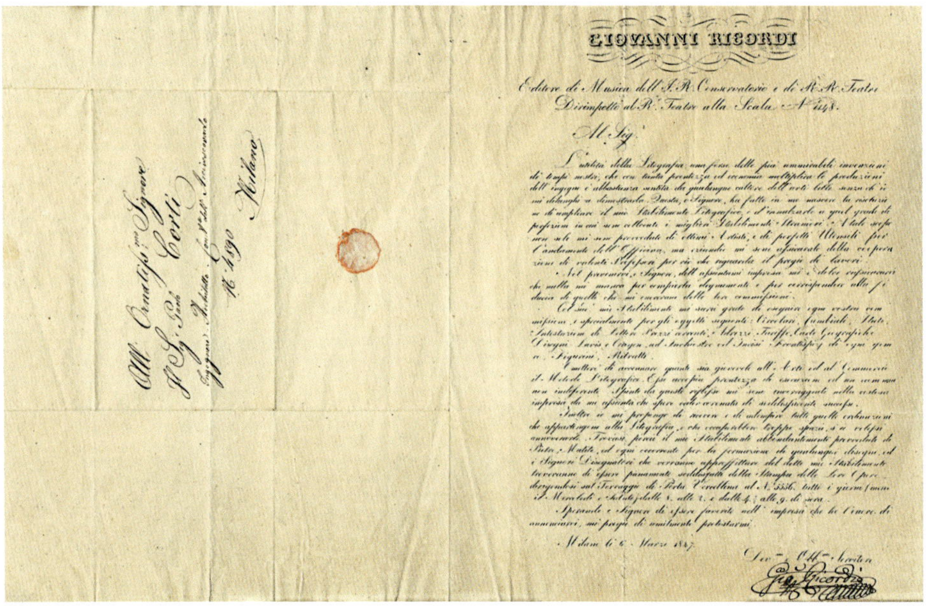

5–8

5—*La Nina pazza per amore* by Giovanni Paisiello, title page of the rental score, manuscript copy

6—Advertising leaflet of Casa Ricordi, 1827

7—First issue of the *Rivista Minima*, periodical published by Casa Ricordi, 1871

8—Ricordi shop, located in the building adjacent to the Teatro alla Scala, lithograph by Alessandro Sanquirico, 1844

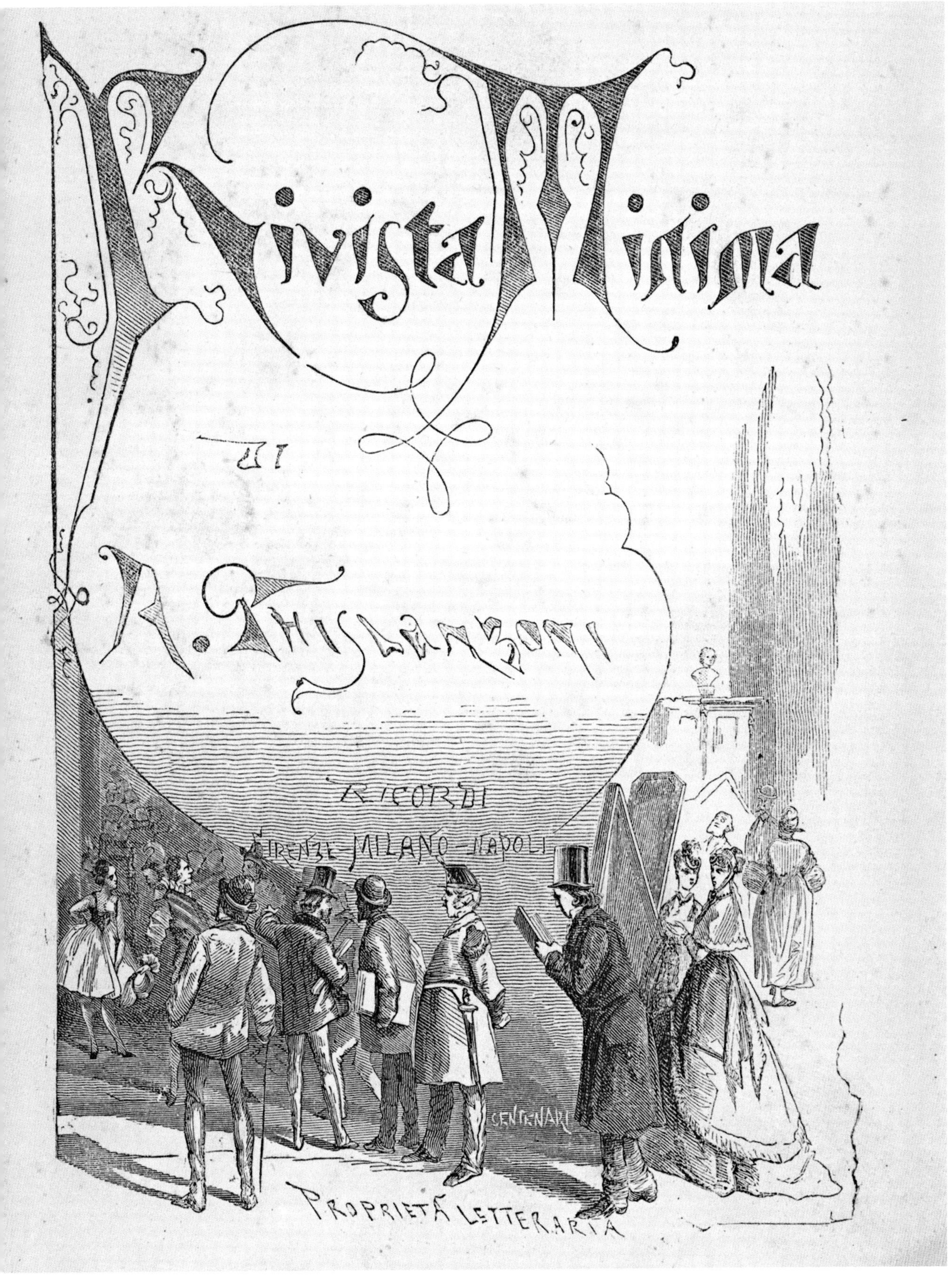
Rivista Minima
di
A. Ghislanzoni
RICORDI
FIRENZE-MILANO-NAPOLI
CENTENARI
PROPRIETÀ LETTERARIA

STABILIMENT

O RICORDI
RICORDI
RARINETTI IN.
CAV. SANQUIRICO D.

2

The Sociable One: Tito I Ricordi

The period from 1853 to 1888

Tito I (1811–1888), who has worked in the business since 1825, takes over as the head of the Ricordi publishing house after Giovanni's death in 1853. It is reported that he was a gentle man in delicate health. His marriage to Giuseppina Arosio is blessed with nine children. He is a draftsman, engraver, printer and a talented pianist. His numerous trips abroad bring him into contact with figures from the European music scene, whom he invites to concerts in Milan – among them Franz Liszt, with whom he is said to have played piano pieces for four hands. In 1863 Tito founds the "Società del Quartetto", still existent, to promote chamber music in the city.

The network of branch offices in Italy and Europe is expanded in Tito's time. The company's partners are the brothers Pietro and Lorenzo Clausetti in Naples and Stefano Jouhaud in Florence, who has worked for Ricordi since 1824. In 1871 Rome becomes the capital of the newly formed Kingdom of Italy, and Ricordi founds a branch there. Tito I Ricordi also proves his political judgment and patriotic spirit by announcing in the *Gazzetta* on June 30, 1861 that he has opened a branch in the "Regno d'Italia". Further branches are set up in London (1878), Palermo and Paris (1888). A new catalog containing 45 000 items is published in 1875.[9] In a letter to the London correspondent Tamplini, Tito I writes confidently: "Dando una scorsa a questo Catalogo si può già comprendere che si tratta del più grande Stabilimento musicale che esista." – "One look at this catalog and one can see that this is the biggest music company there is."[10] During this period, which is characterized by a European financial crisis, Tito I seems to be considering a sale of the company and has it valued: he pegs his profits at over 100 000 lire annually, and the value of the company at two million. Instead of a sale, new strategies for expanding the company's scope for action are developed.

1861

Copyright law has become an important issue since the beginning of the 19th century, and the Ricordi publishing is particularly dedicated to copyright issues specific to the field of music.

In Italy a strong pirate market of scores undermines the author's copyright, as well as the common practice for impresarios to adapt the music to a given performance and its interpreters. Preventing this is in the interests of the Ricordis, whose primary business is the rental of music material for performance.

Casa Ricordi cultivates close ties with its authors and strictly defends their rights, prompting Giuseppe Verdi in 1847 to no longer negotiate with theater impresarios over the rights to his operas, but with the Ricordi publishing house. Giovanni Ricordi himself already experienced several incidents of music piracy: In the cases of *Semiramide* (Rossini) in 1823 and *La Sonnambula* (Bellini) in 1831, this led to pecuniary losses as well as a lowering of artistic standards[11]. Giovanni thinks about ways to prevent this. In the absence of legislation, he initially sees one way forward in signing detailed authors' contracts, and later in their publication in the *Gazzetta* and other important Italian newspapers.

His collaboration with publishers in Europe, for example Boosey in London, also has the aim of preventing music piracy and protecting copyrights. The introduction of legislation is difficult in the pre-unification era (the Risorgimento) because of the country's fragmentation into various dominions. Giovanni Ricordi is one of the three publishers in attendance at talks about a multinational convention at the Milan censorship office in 1839, with representatives from Austria and the Regno di Sardegna[12]. In 1840 an Austro-Sardinian convention is adopted. The copyright protection laid down in it includes works for the theater and also covers piano reductions and arrangements. But asserting the convention proves difficult. The political public is not very interested: the distribution of music lies mainly in the hands of impresarios. Copies and

9—Tito I Ricordi

adaptations are agreed between copyists and theaters. The censorship authorities claim their right to make changes to the content, but are not interested in the matter of rights.

Both Tito I and his son Giulio advocate more extensive legislation. In 1858 Tito I participates in the international congress on copyright regulation in Brussels.[13] Giulio publishes essays on the subject, in which he emphasizes the consequences that arise from violations of the protection of authors' rights: "... in a word: art would have to endure unbearable pain, which cannot be the wish of either the authors or the public in a country as eminently artistic as Italy."[14] With the adoption of the "legge Scialoja" in 1865 and the Berne Convention in 1886, copyright in Italy and Europe is regulated, a process that was decisively helped by members of Casa Ricordi.

1888

Tito I and Giulio's great coup is the acquisition of Francesco Lucca's (the publisher of Wagner in Italy) inventory in 1888 from his widow for the price of one million lire, ending a long-standing rivalry.[15] This also relates to the issue of "Wagner and Verdi" — as a publisher the Ricordi publishing house had always taken a critical stance towards Wagner's work and thus Casa Lucca had obtained the Italian rights.[16] Now, however, the limited partnership "G. Ricordi & C." emerges from the two companies, with 3 800 000 lire in capital. Its shareholders are Tito I and Giulio Ricordi as well as several citizens of Milan: Erminio Bozzotti, Luigi Erba, Francesco Gnecchi, Giuseppe Pisa and Gustavo Strazza.[17] Giulio takes over the management of the company before Tito I dies on September 7, 1888.

10—First issue of the *Giornale della Società del Quartetto*, periodical published by Ricordi under the direction of Tito I, 1864

11—Notification of the Imperial Regio Governo regarding copyrights for literary and artistic works, 1840

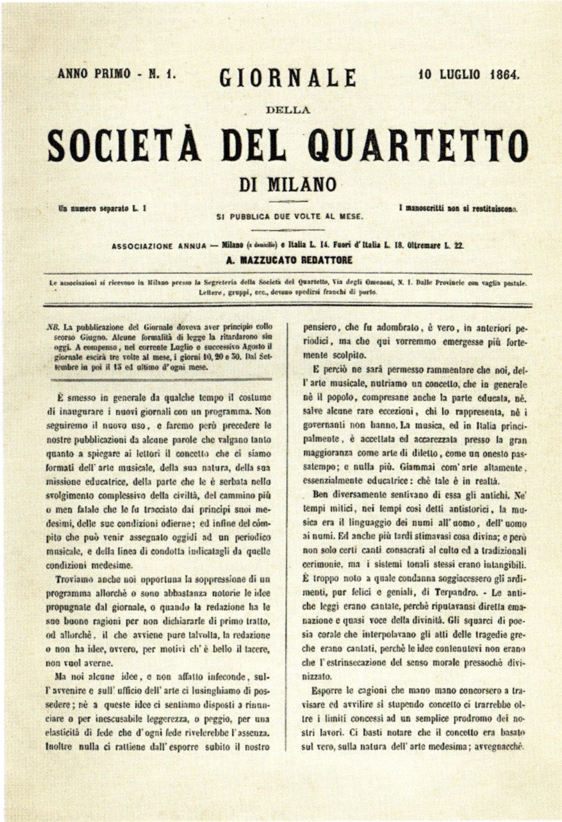

ANNO PRIMO - N. 1. GIORNALE 10 LUGLIO 1864.

DELLA

SOCIETÀ DEL QUARTETTO

DI MILANO

Un numero separato L. 1 — SI PUBBLICA DUE VOLTE AL MESE. — I manoscritti non si restituiscono.

ASSOCIAZIONE ANNUA — Milano (a domicilio) e Italia L. 14. Fuori d'Italia L. 18. Oltremare L. 22.

A. MAZZUCATO REDATTORE

Le associazioni si ricevono in Milano presso la Segreteria della Società del Quartetto, Via degli Omenoni, N. 1. Dalle Provincie con vaglia postale. Lettere, gruppi, ecc., devono spedirsi franchi di porto.

NB. La pubblicazione del Giornale doveva aver principio collo scorso Giugno. Alcune formalità di legge la ritardarono sin oggi. A compenso, nel corrente Luglio e successivo Agosto il giornale escirà tre volte al mese, i giorni 10, 20 e 30. Dal Settembre in poi il 15 ed ultimo d'ogni mese.

È smesso in generale da qualche tempo il costume di inaugurare i nuovi giornali con un programma. Non seguiremo il nuovo uso, e faremo però precedere le nostre pubblicazioni da alcune parole che valgano tanto quanto a spiegare ai lettori il concetto che ci siamo formati dell'arte musicale, della sua natura, della sua missione educatrice, della parte che le é serbata nello svolgimento complessivo della civiltà, del cammino più o men fatale che le fu tracciato dai principi suoi medesimi, delle sue condizioni odierne; ed infine del cómpito che può venir assegnato oggidì ad un periodico musicale, e della linea di condotta indicatagli da quelle condizioni medesime.

Troviamo anche noi opportuna la soppressione di un programma allorchè o sono abbastanza notorie le idee propugnate dal giornale, o quando la redazione ha le sue buone ragioni per non dichiararle di primo tratto, od allorchè, il che avviene pure talvolta, la redazione o non ha idee, ovvero, per motivi ch'è bello il tacere, non vuol averne.

Ma noi alcune idee, e non affatto infeconde, sull'avvenire e sull'ufficio dell'arte ci lusinghiamo di possedere; nè a queste idee ci sentiamo disposti a rinunciare o per inescusabile leggerezza, o peggio, per una elasticità di fede che d'ogni fede rivelerebbe l'assenza. Inoltre nulla ci rattiene dall'esporre subito il nostro pensiero, che fu adombrato, è vero, in anteriori periodici, ma che qui vorremmo emergesse più fortemente scolpito.

E perciò ne sarà permesso rammentare che noi, dell'arte musicale, nutriamo un concetto, che in generale nè il popolo, compresane anche la parte educata, nè, salve alcune rare eccezioni, chi lo rappresenta, nè i governanti non hanno. La musica, ed in Italia principalmente, è accettata ed accarezzata presso la gran maggioranza come arte di diletto, come un onesto passatempo; e nulla più. Giammai com'arte altamente, essenzialmente educatrice: chè tale è in realtà.

Ben diversamente sentivano di essa gli antichi. Ne' tempi mitici, nei tempi così detti antistorici, la musica era il linguaggio dei numi all'uomo, dell'uomo ai numi. Ed anche più tardi stimavasi cosa divina; e però non solo certi canti consacrati al culto ed a tradizionali cerimonie, ma i sistemi tonali stessi erano intangibili. È troppo noto a quale condanna soggiacessero gli ardimenti, pur felici e geniali, di Terpandro. - Le antiche leggi erano cantate, perchè riputavansi diretta emanazione e quasi voce della divinità. Gli squarci di poesia corale che interpolavano gli atti delle tragedie greche erano cantati, perchè le idee contenutevi non erano che l'estrinsecazione del senso morale pressochè divinizzato.

Esporre le cagioni che mano mano concorsero a travisare ed avvilire si stupendo concetto ci trarrebbe oltre i limiti concessi ad un semplice prodromo dei nostri lavori. Ci basti notare che il concetto era basato sul vero, sulla natura dell'arte medesima; avvegnacchè

N.° 26699/3107

IMPERIALE REGIO GOVERNO DI MILANO.

NOTIFICAZIONE.

Inerendo agli ordini recati dall'ossequiato Dispaccio dell'I. R. Cancelleria Aulica unita in data 12 luglio prossimo passato, n.° 21067-1653, si deduce a notizia del Pubblico la Convenzione stipulata tra S. M. I. R. A. e S. M. il Re di Sardegna in data 22 maggio anno corrente, le cui ratificazioni furono concambiate a Vienna il giorno 10 giugno prossimo passato, concernente la guarentigia dei diritti di proprietà delle opere letterarie ed artistiche pubblicate negli Stati rispettivi.

Milano, il 25 agosto 1840.

IL CONTE DI HARTIG,
GOVERNATORE.

GIUDICI, *Consigliere di Governo.*

Dall'Imperiale Regia Stamperia. Prezzo cent. 5.

11—12

G. RICORDI & C.
MUSICA E PIANOFORTI
RICORDI
MUSICA
BARTOLO
PIANO-FORTI
268
269
PIANOFORTI E MUSICA
G. RICORDI & C.
MUSICA
BARTOLO
PIANO-FORTI
VENDITA E NOLO
MUSICALI
CORDE
ARMONICHE
RICORDI
MUSICA

12—13

Ricordi store in Rome,
late 19th century
12—Exterior
13—Interior

3

The Genius: Giulio Ricordi

The period from 1888 to 1912

Giulio Ricordi (1840–1912) officially takes over management of the company after Tito's death in 1888. In fact, however, Tito had closely involved him in the business much earlier, since his official entry into the company in 1863, and entrusted him with many tasks. Giulio influenced many decisions. Under Giulio's aegis the other arts – especially graphics and the visual arts – come to play a greater role in the company's activities. He paints, plays the piano, and his journalistic bent makes him a strong advocate for the company's periodicals. Above all, however, Giulio is a composer himself, publishing numerous original compositions for the piano, small ensembles and a quite successful operetta, *La secchia rapita*, under the curious pseudonym of Jules Burgmein[18].

Giulio's personality is complex and full of contradictions: he is expelled from his school in 1856 for being rebellious, and makes amends with his father by helping out as a secretary in the company. At barely 20 years of age, he is an ardent patriot for the unification of Italy and volunteers for military service (1859). Much later, he will publish his memoirs from that period under the title *Primavera della vita* (Springtime of Life). In 1862 he marries Giuditta Brivio; the marriage produces six children. Tito I senses his son's potential and encourages him where he can. In 1871, he sends him to Germany to study graphic design and typography. Soon after his return he hands over much of the publishing business to Giulio.

In the company Giulio is initially especially devoted to the magazine, the *Gazzetta*. But above all he becomes the crucial new contact for Casa Ricordi's "flagship" composer Giuseppe Verdi, in whom he sees his musical and national ideals united. Tito recognizes Giulio's skill in communicating with Verdi at an early stage and often involves him in discussions[19].

14—Giulio Ricordi, mixed media, photograph by Carlo de Marchi

After the takeover of the Fondo Lucca, whereby Ricordi eliminated its biggest competitor, further acquisitions follow under Giulio's leadership: Orlando in Naples, Bartolo in Rome, Schmidl in Trieste, Pigna in Milan. This is followed by the opening of new branch offices in Germany, Austria, Hungary and Scandinavia and, in 1911, New York. In 1902 the company moves into new premises on Viale di Porta Vittoria (where the "Officine", the "Workshops", have also resided since 1884). The Ricordi catalog now comprises 110 000 publications.[20] In 1908 Casa Ricordi celebrates its 100th anniversary.

1902

Over the course of 100 years, a small copy workshop has grown into a major music publisher that dominates the market and does business internationally – a symbol of Italian music and all of Italian music publishing.

In his centenary speech, Giulio speaks of the emblem of the publisher, the three linked but independent rings or circles ("tre cerchi"; a pre-Renaissance design known as "Borromean Rings"), which are a symbol of unity and power ("l'unione e la forza"). The logo with the added slogan "Ars et Labor" had been created around 1875: Giulio Ricordi's letterhead to Tamplini in London on February 10, 1875 bears the emblem, as does the frontispiece of *Rivista Minima* (which Antonio Ghislanzoni edited) from the same year. Around the turn of the century, the "three rings" are cleverly used on scores, piano and libretti, each artistically incorporated into the graphics. These graphic works make it easy to understand the success with which Casa Ricordi's Officine Grafiche continued to develop the design of their products.

When Giuseppe Verdi's creative energy starts to wane, Giulio puts his good instincts and great knowledge of the music market to use and sets out in search of a new star. As a brilliant publisher impresario, he has by now expanded and secured Ricordi's preeminence in the field of music publishing. Those who are published by him have good career prospects and are also in good hands, because Giulio selflessly cares for his authors once he has made up his mind about someone. He is the "kingmaker"[21] of the Italian music scene of the time. And with a keen sense for musical talent, he promotes the aging Verdi alongside young Giacomo Puccini, whose rise to world fame is significantly precipitated and shaped by Giulio: "We feel Puccini has this precious quality of having IDEAS of his own: and this is something you either have or don't have ..."[22] Giulio supports Puccini emotionally and financially, helps him get through personal and professional crises, accompanies him to premieres, and corresponds with him extensively. Giulio Ricordi, sophisticated and kind in nature, a brilliant entrepreneur with multiple talents, leads the Ricordi publishing house to the zenith of its success. In 1910 new and larger production facilities and warehouses are constructed on Viale Lombardia (now Viale Campania). 70 percent of La Scala's business is conducted with Ricordi; the sales volume of contracts signed by the publisher are triple what they were in the 1860s.[23]

15—17

15—Giuseppe Verdi, Giulio Ricordi, and the painter Carlo Chessa in the garden of Giulio Ricordi's residence in Via Borgonuovo, Milan, photograph by Achille Ferrario, 1892
16—Ricordi store in New York, 1911
17—The historic Ricordi logo over time

G. Ricordi & C.
NEW YORK
G. Ricordi & C.
MILAN

1880s

1890s

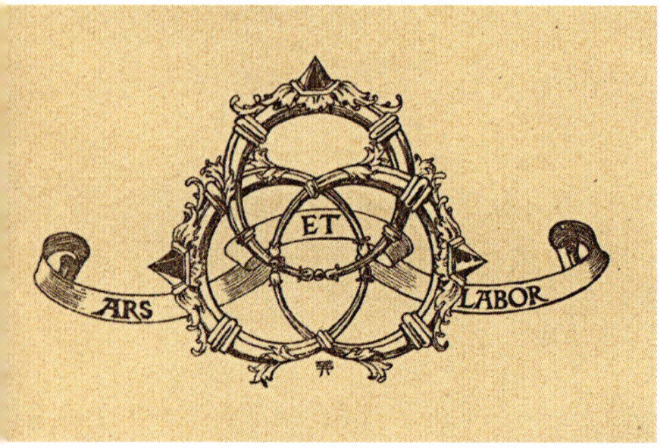

1900s

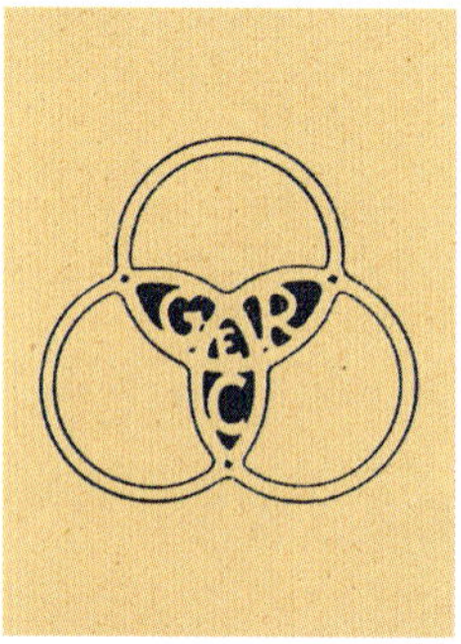

1910s

1920s

1930s

4

The Cosmopolitan: Tito II Ricordi

The period from 1912 to 1919

In keeping with the family tradition, Giulio's eldest son Tito II (1865—1933) is also involved in the publishing business at an early stage — in 1889, immediately after completing his studies. Tito's brother Emanuele (known as Manolo) had already taken over as head of the Officine Grafiche workshop in 1910. But the working relationship between Giulio and Tito II turns out to be conflict-prone.

The times have changed: after the exuberance of nation building, Europe is facing a crisis, and much is being put to the test in the arts as well. The "New World" of America with its ideas and social systems is increasingly penetrating art and life in Europe. And the European art scene is also reinventing itself to a huge degree. Giulio, a 19th-century man through and through, and a proponent of "italianità", cannot quite cope with it. His son Tito II is open to the new forms and new media; he travels a great deal and pushes for changes in the company. Under Manolo's direction the Officine achieve a prominent role in commercial art. In his monograph on the 150th anniversary of the publishing house, Claudio Sartori, the well-known musicologist, writes: "The publisher-patron of the 19th century who holds all the reins of the company in his hands is disappearing. People have changed, times have changed, and the company has grown so large that a distribution of tasks would have become unavoidable in any case."[24]

1910

The reins of the publishing company remain in Giulio's hands, and this leads to considerable tension between father and son, culminating in a rift in February 1907. Giulio is furious about what he considers to be Tito's wastefulness, cavalier attitude and willingness to take risks with money. A letter from Giulio to Tito documents in almost operatically dramatic fashion how disappointed Giulio is with his son's business conduct. He uses language that is reminiscent of a 19th-century libretto.[25]

18—Tito II Ricordi, photograph by Oreste Bertieri, early 20th century

Tito II's merits and qualities are perhaps often forgotten because of this row. After all, he lives in a time in which changes in society and art inevitably affect the business practices of a company like Ricordi. Giulio had taken over the company during the upswing after the Risorgimento, and thereafter led it through steady growth to its economic peak. The discovery and commercialization of Giacomo Puccini, whom he supervised and nurtured like a caring father, is both a symptom and cause of this. As an artist, too, Giulio is still a man of the 19th century: his known compositions are a living testimony of how he absorbed and brilliantly transposed the musical idioms he identified with, those of Verdi, Schumann, Schubert and the French late Romantic period. By contrast, Tito II represents the crisis-ridden character of the turn of the century. With him "the nervousness of the new century"[26] enters the company.

In Italy, the agricultural society — especially in the North — is gradually being replaced by the industrial society, followed by transnational political and social changes, the first waves of emigration from Italy to North and South America as a result of the economic crisis (a crisis that was not preceded by any real upswing after the Risorgimento); a weakening of traditional class distinctions and gender roles; and technical innovations, such as the expansion of the railway network which increases opportunities for travel. This leads to the development of new trends in the arts as well, which can be described as the "courage to embrace subjectivity"[27] and which for Italy can be circumscribed using the poles of art and psychoanalysis (Pirandello/Svevo) versus Dannunzianesimo/Futurism (D'Annunzio/Marinetti).

The translated works of Sigmund Freud appear in Italy and influence one group, while the other group pursues poetics based on technology and progress (including human progress).

Does Giulio remain rooted in the 19th century and the foundations of bourgeois society following liberal patriotism? Is Tito too much of a child of his time, becoming incapable of action by personally experiencing the crisis of the modern subject, or is he the one who, by identifying with the new social and artistic impulses, is open to or at least striving to be open to new strategies and developments, including in his own sphere of influence?

Tito II is born in 1865. In 1889 he completes a degree in engineering, but then devotes himself solely to his father's company. He also plays the piano, is sensitive and witty, and knows how to comport himself in society. Having lost his wife early, he travels a lot: to France, Germany, England and America, where he picks up ideas from the business sector and from theater companies[28]. He reports to his father Giulio on a performance of *Die Meistersinger* in London, acts as the stage director for Puccini's *Tosca*, is responsible for clarifying the rights to the works of Wagner in Italy with Breitkopf & Härtel in Leipzig, which leads to the opening of a branch of Casa Ricordi in that city[29], and lobbies within the company for its participation in the emerging musical reproduction industry. He introduces new technical and artistic ideas to the company, for example color lithography. Succeeding his father, Tito looks after Puccini: he organizes his trip to the Bayreuth Festival, supports him emotionally after the *Madama Butterfly* fiasco (1904) and accompanies him to New York in 1910 for the premiere of *La Fanciulla del West*[30]. But he also adds young composers of his time to the program: Riccardo Zandonai, Franco Alfano and Italo Montemezzi. Like them, Tito is close to the poetics of D'Annunzio, is actively interested in production issues, and later acts as the librettist for *Francesca da Rimini* (Zandonai, 1914) and *La Nave* (Montemezzi, 1918)[31].

The discussion of how the company should respond to the invention of wax cylinders, shellac records and the cinematograph and the arrival of these innovations on the Italian market, appears to have been the first reason for the rift between father and son[32], because Giulio largely refuses to respond entrepreneurially. But sloppy calculations and billing also incited Giulio's displeasure. Baia Curioni hypothesizes that Giulio is interested primarily in the continuity of the company and its commitment to Italian musical heritage, and that he fails to realize that this very goal could be pursued by taking up the technical innovations[33]. As a consequence of the dispute with Tito, in February 1907 Giulio revokes Tito's access to the company's accounts and subjects him to tight monitoring in the company with regard to his expenses — such as for travel. After Giulio's aforementioned bitter letter to his son dated July 5, 1907, Tito II withdraws from the company until his father's death. "[...] del figlio Tito non si parla più" — "there is no more talk about the son Tito",[34] and so any discussions about technical innovations in the music business are also shelved.

19—Tito II Ricordi, early 20th century

After the death of Giulio Ricordi on June 6, 1912 (an event considered so momentous in the world of music lovers that his obituary received a full column in the *New York Times*),[35] however, Tito II becomes head of Casa Ricordi, and has the difficult task of leading the company through the crisis of World War I. The spirit of optimism that was triggered by the new directions the publisher had taken in technical production and artistic terms is extinguished. Tito turns his attention, among other things, to getting into the movie business. But the outbreak of the war and possibly his weaknesses as a businessman prevent any concrete results here. In 1919, he steps down as head of the publishing company because of yet another financial inaccuracy that causes concerns on the supervisory board. So, 111 years after the publishing house was founded, the continuous thread of management by the Ricordi family ends.

1912

Various factors that are related to these family problems only to a limited extent probably result in weakening the publisher's position during the first decade of the 20th century. External circumstances

A Tito Ricordi –
più che all'editore, all'amico e fratello
nelle lotte dell'Arte
Riccardo Zandonai
Milano novembre 1912

20—21

include the political and economic crisis and the war. But the success of a competing publishing house, Sonzogno, founded in 1874, also threatens Casa Ricordi's position. In 1890 Sonzogno publishes Mascagni's *Cavalleria Rusticana* and in 1892 *Pagliacci* by Leoncavallo. It subsequently promotes Italian opera verismo and makes it popular. While Ricordi does celebrate successes with Puccini on the international stage, his work is both traditional and daring, and gets a popular competitor in the lurid modernist verismo works, which are more imbued with national local color. Giulio's response is to further intensifying Ricordi's focus on the country's musical legacy, while Tito II's is to set new accents for the young generation by searching for new voices in contemporary art movements: the musical avant-garde, who are beginning to have an impact with the Second Viennese School (Schönberg, Webern, Berg); the Futurism movement (the first Futurist Manifesto by FT Marinetti is published in *Le Figaro* in Paris in February 1909), which also extends to music; and the classically oriented "dell'Ottanta" generation: Alfano, Casella, Malipiero, Pizzetti, Respighi[38]. The musical world is beginning to diversify, and Ricordi's publishing decisions are no longer as clearly defined and carefully considered as in Giulio's time. The Archivio Storico Ricordi houses the documents: works, librettos, correspondence, and photographs that document these years of change and shed light on the ambivalent figure of Tito II[39] and Casa Ricordi's relationship with the international music scene.

In one matter, the Ricordi publishing house developed a whole new line of business through its sister company, the Officine: graphic reproduction for advertising. Imaginative cover designs are one of Giulio's hobbyhorses: depending on the theme of the opera, he has the covers of its scores and librettos designed in a varied way, with rich ornamentation and illustrations including brilliant variations on the famous "three rings" logo. For each opera a specific graphic look is developed, which is consistently used across all print products.

20—Riccardo Zandonai, photograph with dedication to Tito II Ricordi, 1912

21—Gabriele D'Annunzio, photograph by Varischi & Artico, early 20th century

A major new line of business emerges at the beginning of the new century from the Art Nouveau movement, which flowers in Italy under the concept of "Liberty". Speaking of graphic repro: Officine Grafiche, founded in 1884, develops into a leading European printer. Printing of musical scores, piano reductions and popular editions forms the largest part of its production, but it also develops a standalone graphic arts department: large posters for opera performances, as well as for companies like Campari and major newspapers including the *Corriere della Sera*, and later for movies such as *Cabiria* — even such legendary advertising posters as those for "Bitter Campari" and "Birra Poretti". The team of illustrators includes major artists such as Adolf Hohenstein, Leopoldo Metlicovitz and Marcello Dudovich, who today are considered to be among the "fathers of modern Italian poster design". The Ricordi graphics department is also active in the postcard business.[40] The Archivio Storico Ricordi has an extensive collection from this department.

22–23

22—Tito II Ricordi (second from left) at the opening of the factory Fabbrica Italiana Rulli Sonori Traforati ("F.I.R.S.T.") in Cremona, October 24, 1908

23—Poster by Giovanni Beltrami for the Milanese newspaper *Corriere della Sera*, 1898

GB
CORRIERE DELLA SERA
MILANO VIA PIETRO VERRI 14.
ABBONAMENTI: ANNO L.40-SEM.E L.20-TRIM.E L.10.-
ECCEZIONALI PREMI AGLI ABBONATI
MILANO OFFICINE G. RICORDI & C.

24—25

24—Poster by Loris Riccio for Gi.vi.emme cosmetic powders, 1920

25—Adolf Hohenstein, first art director of the Officine Ricordi, with wife in his studio in Bonn, 1905

5

Years of Crisis: Carlo Clausetti and Renzo Valcarenghi

The period between 1919 and 1943

1919

After the departure of Tito II, management of the publishing company is transferred to Renzo Valcarenghi and Carlo Clausetti, who jointly determine the fortunes of the publishing house from 1919 to 1940. Clausetti comes from a Neapolitan family of publishers and has headed the Ricordi branch office in Naples since 1892. He is similarly as extensively gifted as Giulio Ricordi, works as a composer, music critic, poet and librettist and, with his wife Margherita, entertains a musical salon at his home, where he receives Mascagni, Puccini, Giordano, Tosti, and many other artists of his time. He is a music writer, writing analyses of Wagner's *Tristan und Isolde* and *Götterdämmerung* among other works. Much like Tito II, he is interested in the stage direction of operas, and works on productions of Puccini's *La Fanciulla del West* as "direttore di scena", making sure that the publisher's guidelines are put into practice.

Renzo Valcarenghi joined the company in 1880, and ran the Ricordi branch in Palermo from 1888 to 1912, then the one in Naples. In 1919 he moves to Milan to take over the directorate of Ricordi as administrative manager alongside Clausetti. He lives in the company's headquarters and guides the company through the turbulent years of transition with his calm manner and unconditional loyalty. For many years he serves as president of the Italian Association of Music Publishers and Retailers (Associazione Italiana degli Editori e Negozianti di Musica) and the Publishing Rights Society SIDE (Società Incassi Diritti Editoriali).

It is a time of upheaval in many ways. The "age of technological reproducibility of works of art" (Walter Benjamin) has definitively begun, and radically changes the way music is received. The decline in the practice of amateurs making music in the home, as music can be heard on the radio and records, is just one aspect of this. But this also leads to a decline in the demand for piano reductions and individual songs extracted from the scores (arias, duets), and editions for small ensembles. Because the printing of piano reductions has become one of the cornerstones of the company alongside the rental of music material for performance, this development also has implications for the Ricordi publishing house.

26—Renzo Valcarenghi, manager of Casa Ricordi, early 20th century

27—Carlo Clausetti, manager of Casa Ricordi, early 20th century

Studies of documents in the Archivio Ricordi provide information about Ricordi during the fascist period (1922–1943), for example of correspondence and publishing catalogs before 1931 (the later years no longer exist).[41] Casa Ricordi's relationship with the fascist regime is gradually formed through its participation in committees (Renzo Valcarenghi represents the publishers in the Consiglio della Corporazione dello Spettacolo [Council of the guild of the theater]), the acceptance of censorship[42] and, far worse in human terms, the naming of Jewish authors after the introduction of the National Socialist racial laws in Italy in 1938.[43] By cooperating, Casa Ricordi safeguards its opportunities for revenue from music rental fees and collection on authors' rights.

1923

Despite this cooperation, which appears to be limited to formal aspects, the members of Casa Ricordi have an ambivalent relationship to fascism. For example, Renzo's son Aldo Valcarenghi is involved in a defense campaign for Arturo Toscanini after the "slapping" affair in Bologna in May 1931. Toscanini had been attacked and beaten by some fascists because he refused to open a concert in Bologna with the fascist anthem "Giovinezza".[44] Some students responded by distributing leaflets in his defense. In 1938 the young Pietro Clausetti sets some passages from a speech by Mussolini to music in an "Inno all'Impero", which is presented to the Duce.[45] However, this "homage" is not well received, as the work is in competition with the "Inno imperiale", featuring a text from Achille Starace, secretary of the Fascist Party. Starace has

La Fiamma.
Un gruppo di funzionari.
atto 3°
Nicola Benois
33.

all copies of the Clausetti anthem removed from stores in Rome.[46]

The reading of business correspondence ("Copialettere") from those years has yet to shed more light on Casa Ricordi's ties to the fascist regimes, which are characterized by making certain concessions to gain autonomy and scope for action.

Another area of change concerns the position of the theaters, and their relationship with the publisher. They have become autonomous institutions, and during the fascist period become increasingly subject to the orders of the responsible ministry (Ministero per la Stampa e la propaganda)[47]. While La Scala occupies first place among the subsidized theaters from 1923, the state's interest in the theater is as a means to spread regime-conformist propaganda and teachings.[48]

The development of musical aesthetics in Italy is subject to these external conditions: The focus is on functionalizing all performances for propaganda purposes in the spirit of an italianità now dominated by fascism.[49] While on the one hand there are backward-looking, neoclassical and neoromantic tendencies (especially in instrumental music), a musical avant-garde is also active on two levels: on one level, the Futurist movement gives rise to a musical aesthetic direction leaning toward music and technology, and music and noise (e.g. replicating the acoustic settings of cities or factories). On another level, a small group of authors takes up the aesthetics of the Viennese avant-garde and transposes them in a way that is oriented to the Italian primacy of melody. The theater, squeezed between censorship and demands for innovation, takes a "keep a stiff upper lip" approach and produces opera classics and moderately modern works.

28—*La fiamma* by Ottorino Respighi, world premiere, Rome, Teatro dell'Opera, 1934. A group of officers, Act III, costume design by Nicola Benois

29—*Volo di notte* by Luigi Dallapiccola, title page of the draft libretto with the stamp of the fascist theatrical censorship of the Ministero della Cultura Popolare, 1939

Casa Ricordi seems to come to terms with these new conditions. The composers of the popular "Giovane Scuola" (with Mascagni as the main representative) is published by its competitor Sonzogno, and a "successor" to Puccini has not yet been found. Besides Italo Montemezzi and Franco Alfano, the Ricordi catalogs of the 1920s list the work of other members of the "dell'Ottanta" generation, later followed by composers such as Erich Wolfgang Korngold, Mario Castelnuovo-Tedesco and Aldo Finzi. Collaboration with La Scala becomes difficult, but Casa Ricordi retains some influence. From 1921–1929 Arturo Toscanini is La Scala's musical director and puts his stamp on the selection. Naturally, he is increasingly struggling with the regime and its ideological dictates. In

1928

28–29

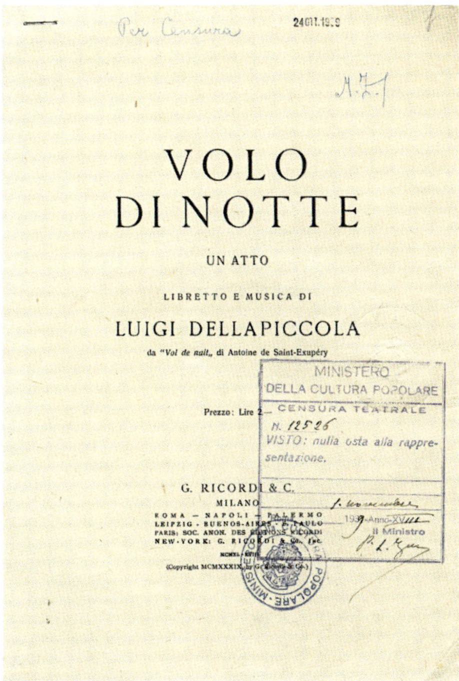
Per Censura

VOLO
DI NOTTE

UN ATTO

LIBRETTO E MUSICA DI

LUIGI DALLAPICCOLA

da "Vol de nuit" di Antoine de Saint-Exupéry

MINISTERO
DELLA CULTURA POPOLARE
CENSURA TEATRALE
N. 12526
VISTO: nulla osta alla rappresentazione.
Il Ministro

G. RICORDI & C.
MILANO
ROMA – NAPOLI – PALERMO
LEIPZIG – BUENOS-AIRES – S. PAULO
PARIS: SOC. ANON. DES EDITIONS RICORDI
NEW-YORK: G. RICORDI & CO. (INC.)

addition to a classical repertoire, the works of these Ricordi composers are staged: Boito with *Mefistofele* and *Nerone*, Catalani with *La Wally*, Franchetti with *Cristoforo Colombo* and *Germania* (libretto by Illica), Pizzetti with *Debora e Jaele*, Alfano with *La leggenda di Sakùntala*, Casella with *Le couvent sur l'eau* (commedia coreografica), Zandonai with *I cavalieri di Ekebù* and *Francesca da Rimini* (D'Annunzio's version), Wolf-Ferrari with *Le donne curiose* and *Sly*, Montemezzi with *L'amore dei tre re*, an "azione coreografica" entitled *Vecchia Milano* by Giuseppe Adami (music by Franco Vittadini), and Respighi with *La campana sommersa* (by Gerhart Hauptmann). Wagner's "Ring", *Die Meistersinger von Nürnberg*, *Lohengrin* and *Tristan und Isolde*, and various works by Strauss (*Rosenkavalier*, *Salome*) and Humperdinck also appear repeatedly in the repertoire.[50] In the area of "early music" Casa Ricordi successfully stands its ground, for example with the publication of an edition of Antonio Vivaldi's works (edited by Gian Francesco Malipiero), and efforts to promote a performance of Claudio Monteverdi's *Orfeo* in an arrangement by Giacomo Benvenuti.[51]

30–31

The tension between Casa Ricordi and La Scala is exacerbated by the appointment of a Scala director loyal to the regime, Jenner Mataloni. The Casa Ricordi representatives have repeated contentious dealings with him, about income from the performances as well as production conditions — such as the publisher's representatives no longer being allowed to participate in rehearsals — through to outright prohibitions of productions. Mainardi cites the example of the opera *La bisbetica domata* (*The Taming of the Shrew* by Shakespeare) by Mario Persico, whose performance Casa Ricordi prepared for the 1937/1938 season, but which founders due to Mataloni's intervention.[52] Korngold's *Die tote Stadt* is performed at the instigation of Ricordi in the 1938/1939 season, however, at the Teatro dell'Opera in Rome.

At the same time, Casa Ricordi manages to strengthen and expand its international network during the Valcarenghi-Clausetti era: overseas branches are set up in 1924 (Buenos Aires, directed by Guido Valcarenghi, one of Renzo's sons) and in 1927 (São Paulo, led by Giuseppe Giacompol), and the company's volume increases as it buys up various stocks from other publishers in South America.

1938

By 1940, the Ricordi catalog comprises 125 000 items. 260 employees work for the Milan sites in eight departments, and six million pages are printed annually.[53]

Another focus of the publisher's work during these years is the publication of six volumes in a musicological series, the *Istituzioni e Monumenti dell'Arte Musicale Italiana* between 1931 and 1939, under the direction of Gaetano Cesari and, after his

30—Aldo Finzi, circa 1930
31 —Italo Montemezzi with Sem Benelli and Franco Alfano, photograph by Attilio Badodi, early 20th century

death, Guido Pannain. The series focuses on the music of the 16th century: Andrea and Giovanni Gabrieli, Camerata Fiorentina and Claudio Monteverdi, Carlo Gesualdo and others. Mainardi calls the series "one of the first major products of Italian musicology".[54] This is uncharted territory for the publisher,[55] and marks its entry into the incipient discipline of musicology in Italy. Given its successful *Gazzetta Musicale* and subsequent publications — including *Musica d'Oggi* from 1919 — this is consistent with the publisher's policy.

In 1940 Carlo Clausetti leaves the company and is replaced by Alfredo Colombo. The dual leadership of Renzo Valcarenghi/Colombo lasts four years. The offices, production facilities, and the warehouses and rental libraries of Casa Ricordi are badly damaged during the bombing of Milan on August 13, 1943: two bombs fall on the publisher's headquarters in Via Berchet, and incendiary bombs fall into the buildings on Viale Campania.[56] Parts of the archive are destroyed. In 1942 the most valuable documents of the archive had already been moved to secure locations: the autograph music scores, for instance, to the underground air raid shelters of the Cassa di Risparmio bank in Milan and of the Conservatory of Parma, as well as to directors' houses on Lake Maggiore, Lake Como and near Varese. Duplicates of the printed scores are brought to safety as master copies. The library and much of the rental material, including some editions with unique handwritten changes, are irretrievably destroyed in the attack. As a result, the works of many composers, too expensive (or impossible) to reconstruct after the war, are forgotten.

1943

The scores and letters, the libretto collection and also the picture archive are spared. But shaken by the loss after many years of great crisis, Valcarenghi resigns in 1944. A three-person management is now set up, ensuring family continuity as before — albeit no longer limited to the Ricordi family: Alfredo Colombo, Eugenio Clausetti (another son of Carlo) and Camillo Ricordi (the son of Manolo Ricordi). These three manage the reconstruction and rebuilding of the archive.

32, 33—Bombing of the Ricordi production offices in Viale Campania, August 13, 1943

34—36

The Ricordi offices in
Viale Campania
34—A typesetter at work
35—Machine room
36—Binding room

L. VAN BEETHOVEN
SONATE
PER PIANOFORTE

6

The Postwar Years

The period from 1943 to 1956

In the years after the war, Casa Ricordi has to struggle to keep up, as the publisher has to upgrade its inventory to meet the market's demands. In keeping with the company's tradition, this is done partly by purchasing other inventories (Mario Pasquariello in Naples, Romero y Fernandez in Buenos Aires, where a branch had already been founded in 1924), and also by successively establishing new branches and sales and representation agencies or expanding existing ones: in Genoa (1953), Toronto (1954), Sydney (1956) Palermo (1957), and Mexico City (1958). A small part of the library is reacquired through donations. In 1950, the new store opens in the reconstructed building on Via Berchet. In 1952 the company is converted into a limited liability company, with Alfredo Colombo as president and Guido Valcarenghi and Eugenio Clausetti as managing directors. In 1956 it becomes a stock corporation, whose executive board includes the three men named above as well as other personalities.[57]

Above all, the situation for music publishers has changed and hence the role and standing of Ricordi. The postwar period is characterized by a process that had been emerging since the introduction of the technology to reproduce music early in the 20th century: the separation of "light" and "serious" music. Put bluntly, light ("popular") music has become a mass phenomenon, while serious music is marginalized.

Ricordi responds by entering into the popular music business, founding "Radio Record Ricordi" ("RRR") in 1948 and a year later the monthly newsletter *Rassegna Musicale Radio Record Ricordi*. The management of Radio Record Ricordi is taken over by Mariano Rapetti, a pianist and songwriter ("paroliere"), who has already been an employee of the company for several years. His son Giulio, also a lyricist, will go on to form a legendary writing team under the pseudonym Mogol in the 1960s with the "cantautore" Lucio Battisti. The foundation of "Fono Film Ricordi", and later "Edir" and "Ritmi e Canzoni" also lay the cornerstone for the later establishment of "Dischi Ricordi" by Carlo Emanuele Ricordi, also known as Nanni, in 1958.

37—Presentation of the movie *Casa Ricordi*, directed by Carmine Gallone, at Cinema Orfeo in Genoa, 1954

The years 1943 to 1956 are not well documented in terms of the publisher's history. In particular, there is a lack of publishing catalogs. A thorough review of the business correspondence ("copialettere") and sifting through any publishing catalogs that can still be retrieved would be a worthwhile task and would fill an important gap.

38—41

38—Entrance of the Ricordi headquarters in Via Berchet, Milan, before 1959
39—Ricordi store in Genoa, circa 1950
40—Ricordi offices in Sydney, waiting room, mid-20th century
41—Carlo Emanuele Ricordi, a.k.a. Nanni, circa 1950

7

Il mio ufficio
è al 30°
piano dove
la finestra
è aperta
e comprende
nove
finestre
(5 sulla 51 St.
e 4 sulla 6 Av.)

A Time of Change

The period from 1956

With the conversion of the Ricordi publishing house to a stock corporation in 1956, a period of consolidation begins. Two priorities determine the following period in the publisher's history: the formation of the generation of "cantautori" (the word is usually translated as "singer-songwriters", but actually means "bards") and serious contemporary music. The Ricordi publishing house helps launch the cantautori through the creation of Dischi Ricordi in early 1958, under the management of Nanni Ricordi. Much like it did in the 19th century, during the grandfather's generation, the publishing house now plays a decisive role in establishing and promoting an important part of Italian culture. Perhaps the same familial instinct is at work here?

1956

In his foreword to a monograph with memories of Nanni Ricordi, which is published in 2010 at the instigation of his cousin (3rd degree removed) Claudio Ricordi, he calls this instinct "the right balance between important cultural production and brilliant entrepreneurship [...]".[58] From this volume of memoirs, in which the main cantautori represented by Ricordi also have their say, it is clear that in his grandfathers' tradition, Nanni embraces a principle that helped the publisher to success and recognition in the 19th century: discovering new authors and providing support in a close publisher-author relationship. But it is above all also a technical innovation that leads to success: the spread of the 'single record' developed by RCA Victor, played at 45 rpm instead of 33 rpm.[59]

Nanni is born in 1932 and studies law in Milan and piano on the side, initially as a hobby, but then ever more intensively, so that he finally passes an exam at the conservatory. While working at the SIAE (Società Italiana degli Autori ed Editori) in Rome he gets to know Luchino Visconti, Maria Callas and others during his frequent visits to the theater and opera, and gets a feel for the music scene. Then he and Franco Colombo jointly head Ricordi's New York branch for several years. Here, he gains important impetus from meeting various artistic figures — including Gian Carlo Menotti, Marilyn Monroe and Leonard Bernstein — which he channels into the establishment of Dischi Ricordi after his return to Italy. Above all, the New York scene teaches him to reconsider the strict separation of serious and popular music that has become established in Europe.

42—Ricordi offices in New York, mid-20th century

In 1957 the first Ricordi record is produced at La Scala: the opera *Medea* by Cherubini with Maria Callas in the title role. Nanni has equipment brought over from the legendary Mercury company in New York (which today represents Elton John, Mariah Carey and Lionel Richie among others) and devotes himself to the recording technology and production conditions with great expertise.[60] The result is a recording that still has an amazing "presence", a "tinta scenica" (dramatic mood), "as loved by Verdi".[61]

After the success of the Medea recording, which was published on the occasion of the 150th anniversary of Casa Ricordi, Nanni works on profitably expanding record production. He has in mind the popular music that, despite the efforts of Mariano Rapetti, has been rather neglected by the publishing company until now. Inspired by the French chansons that have come into fashion (Brassens, Brel), and the Anglo-Saxon pop-rock wave, he goes talent hunting in Milan. In the central Milan club Santa Tecla he meets a guitarist called Giorgio Gaberscik and encourages him to compose his own songs. Under the name of Giorgio Gaber, he becomes Dischi Ricordi's first cantautore. Nanni aims to revolutionize the old-fashioned taste of the traditional song festival in Sanremo, and to get away from national styles or genre boundaries: "The difficulty was to find music that would stand the test of time and was exportable, while still being a consumer product like *Traviata*

1958

43–45

43—Nanni Ricordi and Maria Callas during the gala celebration of Casa Ricordi's sesquicentennial, Milan, 1958

44—Giancarlo Menotti, circa 1950

45—Tullio Serafin conducting the studio recording of *Medea* by Luigi Cherubini at the Teatro alla Scala, first record issued by Dischi Ricordi to celebrate the sesquicentennial of Casa Ricordi, at the music stand Maria Callas, 1957

was in its day".[62] In the following years Dischi Ricordi publishes the songs of Gino Paoli, Luigi Tenco, Ornella Vanoni, Enzo Jannacci, Lucio Battisti, Fabrizio De André and many others.[63] Nanni and his wife Marisa also continue the tradition of the Ricordi salons in their own way: they receive artists from all disciplines at their house for festive evenings of eating, drinking and playing music.[64]

But despite the success of Dischi Ricordi, the Ricordi publishing house (now with new production offices, which were moved from Viale Campania to Via Salomone) never really embraced popular music, which is why in 1963 Nanni Ricordi leaves to join the Italian branch of the American record company RCA in Rome. In 1964, he runs the Festival dei Due Mondi in Spoleto – the Spoleto Festival – where he establishes a concert series with the programmatic title "Bella ciao", which presents traditional Italian folk songs – "Bella ciao" is perhaps the most famous song of the Resistenza.

The basically rather left-leaning political cantautori scene around Nanni Ricordi ideologically relates to the second major focus of the Ricordi publishing house's production in the period from 1958. The Ricordi publishing house becomes the editorial home of leading figures of contemporary music and – after an initially conservative stance – especially for musical theater, which receives crucial impulses for innovation from Italy: Luigi Nono, Bruno Maderna, Luciano Chailly, Luciano Berio, Giacomo Manzoni, Franco Donatoni, Luca Lombardi, Sylvano Bussotti, Azio Corghi, Giorgio Battistelli and Salvatore Sciarrino. It begins its collaboration with festivals in the big cities of Milan, Turin, Bologna and the Music Biennale in Venice, with exchange institutions abroad such as the International Summer Course in Darmstadt and the Donaueschingen Festival. Casa Ricordi's international orientation, which already influenced its 19th century history, now comes into play again in a different guise.

The publishing company maintains branch offices in France (Paris), Great Britain (Chesham near London), Germany (first Lörrach and Frankfurt, then Munich), the United States (New York), Argentina (Buenos Aires) and Brazil (São Paulo). From 1961, it is led by Guido Valcarenghi, followed by Carlo Origoni and in 1982 Gianni Babini. Guido Rignano becomes the managing director in 1964. Under his guidance, the Ricordi publishing company develops strategies aimed at both the broad public taste and the musical elite.

1961

Four main areas of publishing activity begin to emerge. The first priority is reviving the classic Italian opera tradition. The catalog supplements from 1957 to 1966 list numerous scores, piano reductions and individual editions. For example, arias from Verdi's *Un ballo in Maschera, Otello, Falstaff*, Puccini's *Tosca, Madama Butterfly, Manon Lescaut* and Catalani's *La Wally* are republished. The proposition of critical works editions based on the original documents, primarily the autograph scores (Rossini, Verdi, Vivaldi) should be seen in connection with the publisher's attention to tradition. Ricordi's editorial department, led by Luciana Pestalozza from 1964 to 1991 and by Gabriele Dotto from 1992 to 2001, provides decisive impetus. The critical edition of the works of Rossini begins in 1969 with the publication of *Il Barbiere di Siviglia* by the Urbino musicologist and conductor of the New York City Opera Alberto Zedda, a Rossini specialist, and continues with the Fondazione Rossini in Pesaro. The complete critical edition of the works of Verdi is produced as a co-edition with the University of Chicago Press, under the overall direction of the Chicago musicologist Philip Gossett. The first volume is *Rigoletto*, which in 1983 was the basis of a performance at the Vienna State Opera, among others. This is followed by complete editions of the operas of Donizetti (in collaboration with the Fondazione Donizetti of Bergamo and under the direction of Gabriele Dotto and Roger Parker), of the works of Bellini (in collaboration with the Teatro Massimo of Catania and under the direction of Fabrizio Della

46

46—Giorgio Gaber, circa 1960

Seta, Alessandro Roccatagliati and Luca Zoppelli), and of the operas of Puccini (under the direction of Gabriele Dotto), the sonatas of Domenico Scarlatti, and the works of Antonio Vivaldi (in collaboration with the Istituto Italiano Antonio Vivaldi).

Musical education remains another focus of the publishing activity. Many piano tutorials are published, as well as singing guides and introductions to music. In this context the continuation of the Ricordi publishing company's tradition of publishing periodicals and books is also worth mentioning. From 1951, the magazine *Ricordiana* is published (until 1957), *Musica d'Oggi* is revived (1958 to 1965), the *Enciclopedia della Musica* is published in four volumes, and there is a small book series *(Piccola Biblioteca Ricordi)* and a redesigned libretto series.

1969

But serious contemporary music also finds a home in the publishing company, a sector that is mainly promoted by Luciana Pestalozza (who was instrumental in the founding of the influential Milanese concert series "Musica nel nostro tempo" in the mid 1970s) and Mimma Guastoni, who had been an employee of the firm since the 1960s and became a manager in 1981 and managing director from 1995—1998.

Ricordi is still regarded as the leading music publishing company in Italy, especially when it comes to music for the theater: "The theater production market was entirely absorbed by Casa Ricordi".[65] The publisher retains its European orientation, with a strong presence of UK and French composers in its affiliates in London and Paris, but also remains the primary publishing home of Italian composers. In a business where many publishers rarely saw their role as going beyond that of engraving, typesetting and printing, Ricordi instead established a long tradition of highly qualified editors who ensured an exceptional degree of care in the preparation of the editions and who, in many cases, became trusted advisors and collaborators to the composers themselves.

1981

This, together with the extensive distribution network and state-of-the-art printing facilities, became an added advantage in attracting a growing number of composers to the Ricordi catalog. In the 20th century two editors-in-chief (both of them skilled composers, arrangers and edition-curators in their own right) attain almost legendary status among composers and conductors: Raffaele Tenaglia, who worked with Ricordi first as an outside collaborator and then as head of the rental archive and of the editorial and production department from 1913 to 1961 and who was a trusted editor for Puccini. And Fausto Broussard, editor-in-chief from the early 1960s through 1996, whom the young composers of the avant-garde "trusted blindly" (in the words of Luciana Pestalozza), and were "asking for advice while preparing the music and for technical details".[66]

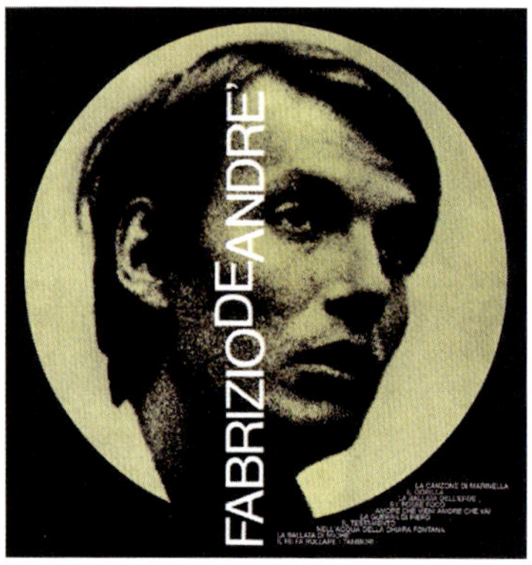

47–53

Ricordi album covers:
47—*Luigi Tenco* by Luigi Tenco, 1962
48—*Il mondo in tasca — Io che sarei* by Gino Paoli, 1967
49—*A che cosa ti serve amare* by Gino Paoli, 1966
50—*Un uomo che vale* by Gino Paoli, 1965
51—*La carta vincente* by Gino Paoli, 1966
52—*Fabrizio De André* by Fabrizio De André, 1968
53—*Una sera con ... Gino Paoli* by Gino Paoli, 1979

54—59

54—Franco Donatoni
55—Bruno Maderna
56—Azio Corghi
57—Luciano Chailly
58—Luigi Nono
59—Luciano Berio

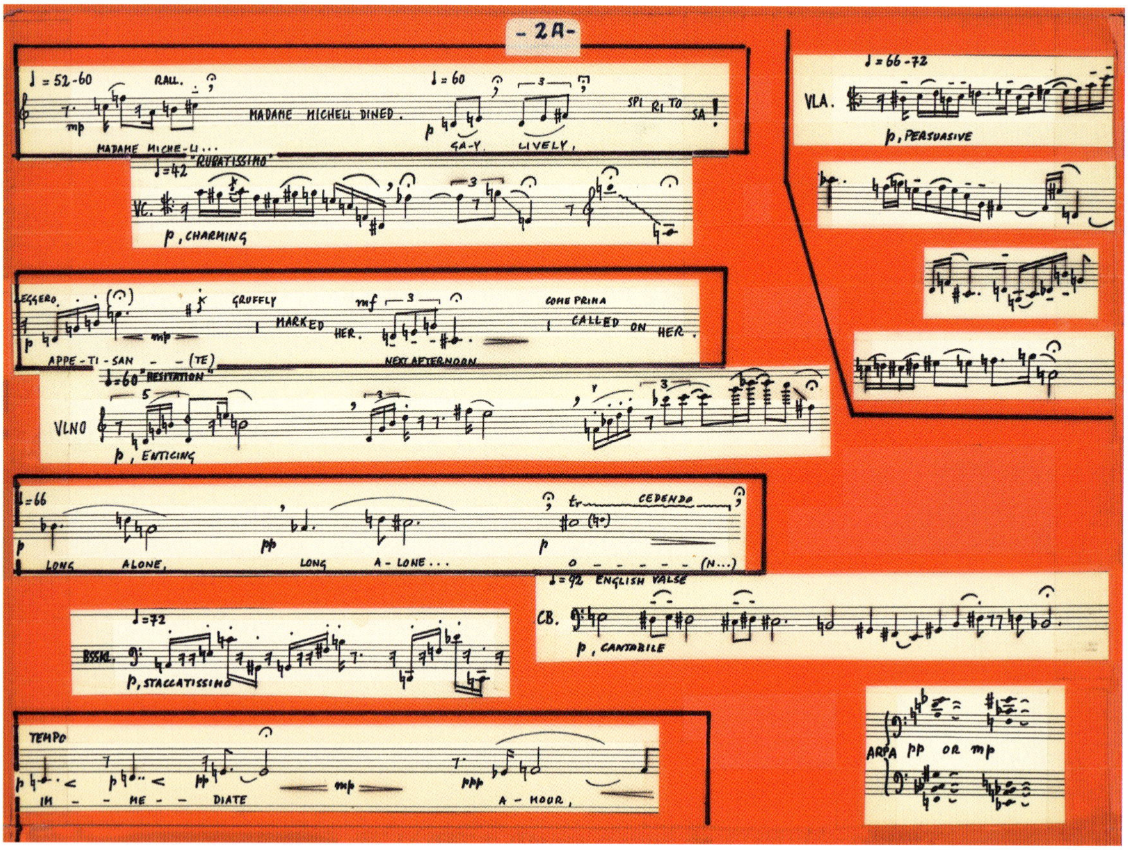

60

Support for new works is carried out on a smaller scale and for a specialist audience, and marketing strategies are geared not toward sales volume, but toward qualitative criteria. Maintaining contacts with the leading music festivals in Italy and elsewhere in Europe becomes a priority, as the performance of contemporary music depends on these dedicated events, which have ties to the ensembles and inspire and organize performances of these highly specialized musical works. The Darmstadt International Summer Course for New Music, which was revived in 1946 by Wolfgang Steinecke, and where courses with composers of international renown alternate with concerts (the holiday courses exist to this day), are an important point of reference for the Ricordi publishing house as well. Its composers are invited as lecturers — and thus as multipliers of a publishing program that is expanding stylistically — and its works are played at the concerts.[67] Among the foreign composers included in the publisher's program are such respected names as Gerard Grisey, Brian Ferneyhough, Magnus Lindberg, Klaus Huber, Younghi Pagh-Paan, Heiner Goebbels, Rolf Riehm, Peter Eötvös and Olga Neuwirth.

60—*Venetian Journal* by Bruno Maderna, autograph score, 1972

In 1994, Ricordi is sold to the Bertelsmann Music Group (BMG), part of the German media group Bertelsmann. At this time, it is the only independent Italian music company that is still able to stand its ground alongside the dominant international majors, led by Polygram, EMI and Warner. In addition to the Italian companies, among them the Arte Grafiche printing plant and the recording-medium business Dischi Ricordi, the group of companies includes holdings in nine other countries. Casa Ricordi is more international than most other companies in classical music publishing. BMG's strategic activities in the years following the acquisition focus mainly on the lucrative music publishing business and on the high-volume business with recording mediums, which is merged with BMG's labels (BMG Ariola Italy). The chain of stores and the attached real-estate holdings are sold off.

1994

In 2006, Bertelsmann sells the Ricordi imprint to the Universal Publishing Music Group, a subsidiary of France's Vivendi Group. It continues the Ricordi publishing program, with offices in Italy. This also opens a new chapter in the history of the Archivio Storico Ricordi. Placed under the protection of Italy's cultural authorities back in 1994, it remains in Bertelsmann's possession, along with the rights to the Ricordi brand. The close collaboration between Casa Ricordi and the Archivio Storico Ricordi continues to this day. Critical editions are still being produced based on it, and help to continually update our view of classical Italian opera.

2006

The fact that the archive was firmly integrated into Ricordi's business processes until the mid-1990s, albeit not indexed from an academic-archival standpoint, requires a new approach. Its transformation from a classical business archive into a modern, historically and creatively usable (research) archive, one that is not restricted to the narrow circle of musicology, has begun.

Based on an ongoing cataloging process, extensive parts of the archive are now being digitized and gradually brought online.[68] Nowadays, the Archivio Ricordi attracts great attention outside Italy as well; not least due to Verdi Year 2013, when it was finally brought to the attention of a wider public in Germany and beyond.

Exhibitions in Berlin, Brussels and Madrid significantly contribute to its international perception, while its integration into the cultural life of Milan is intensified by collaboration with the Teatro alla Scala Museum and other measures. The aim of all these activities is to promote the use of the archive, be it through collaboration with musicologists[69] or licensing agreements with other institutions such as opera houses[70]. In January 2016, a licensing agreement with the Milan fashion house Dolce & Gabbana, which displayed bags based on Ricordi motifs from Puccini operas at the Alta Moda show at La Scala in Milan, caused a stir.[71]

Strange as it may seem for a modern fashion house to decorate its products with costume drawings from the early twentieth century, it demonstrates the inspirational potential of the archive:

2016

The unique link between entrepreneurship and creativity that is reflected in Ricordi's entire company history is ultimately also continued in the archive's "marketing." All revenues generated from licensing or marketing the archive's materials or Ricordi brand are used to safeguard, preserve, and index the archive and make it accessible.

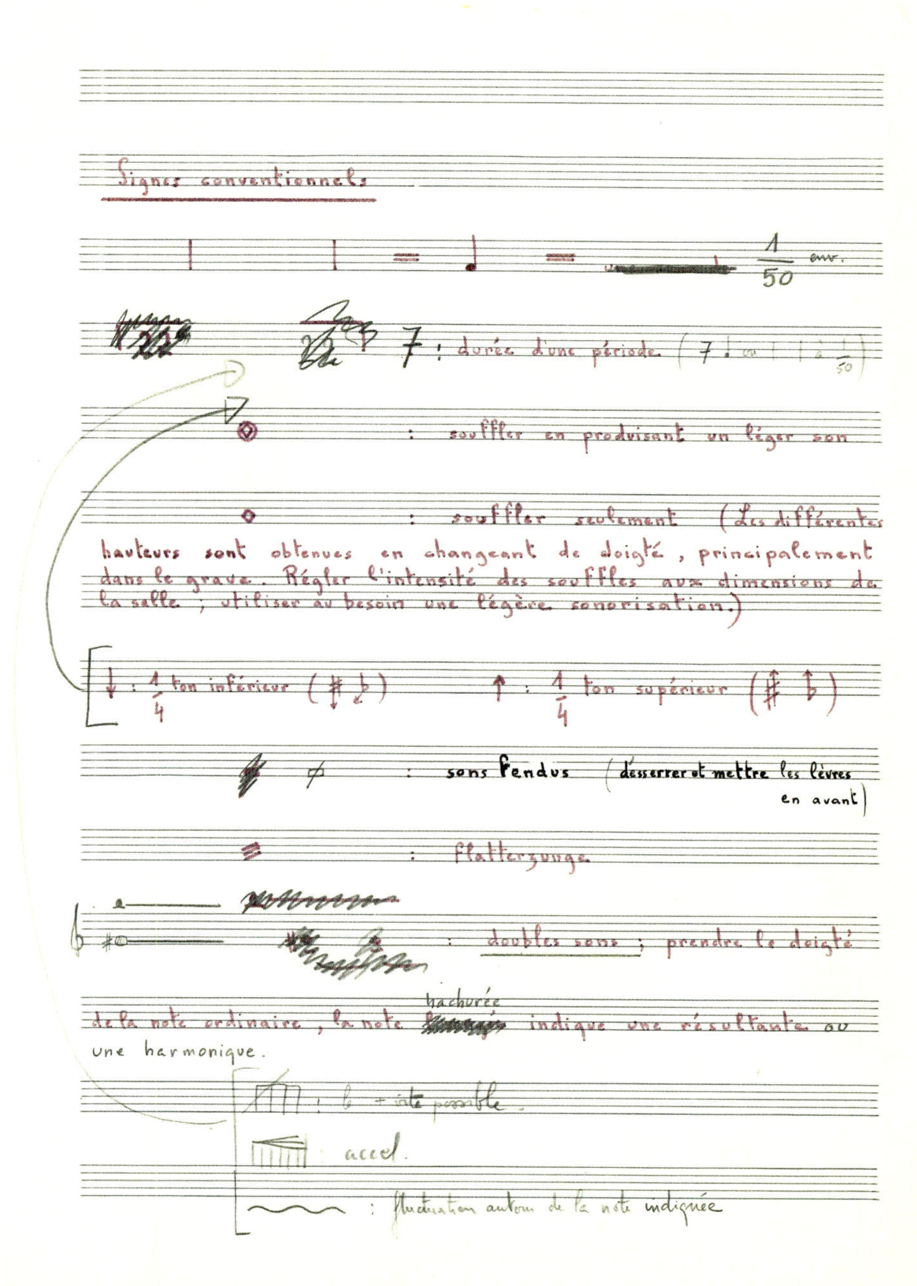

61–62

61—*Charme* by Gérard Grisey, autograph score, 1969
62—Drawing by Guido Crepax for a printed edition of "American Western" style music, 1958

LA GAZZA LADRA

Gioachino Rossini
(1792 - 1868)

Sinfonia

63—64

La Gazza Ladra by
Gioachino Rossini
63—Ricordi critical edition,
Milan, 1979
64—Autograph score, 1817

Footnotes

1

1 —See Marino Berengo, *Intellettuali e librai nella Milano della Restaurazione*, Milan 1980, pp. 1—32.
2 —Cf. Stefano Baia Curioni: *Mercanti dell'opera. Storie di Casa Ricordi*, Milan 2011, p. 49.
3 —Cf. Claudio Sartori, *Casa Ricordi 1808/1958. Profilo storico. Itinerario grafico editoriale*, Milan 1958, p. 22.
4 —Cf. on this process Luke Jensen, *Giuseppe Verdi & Giovanni Ricordi, With Notes on Francesco Lucca. From Oberto to La traviata*, New York and London 1989, pp. 7—9. See also Philip Gossett, *Dive e maestri. L'opera italiana messa in scena*, Milan 2009.
5 —The branches are run with the help of partners, beginning with one Grua in London and Florence, then Pozzi and later Stefano Jouhaud in Florence. Cf. Sartori, p. 31.
6 —The Litografia continues operating until 1895. One of its first major productions was twelve illustrations for the first edition of the novel *The Betrothed* by Alessandro Manzoni 1827. Cf. on this and on the founding of the Litografia Sartori, pp. 32—40.
7 —The 1838 catalog was the last one to have a "promotional" character. Cf. Sartori, p. 41.
8 —Baia Curioni, p. 120.

2

9 —Cf. Sartori, p. 53.
10 —As quoted by Baia Curioni, p. 144, letter, dated January 25, 1876.
11 —Cf. Baia Curioni, pp. 74—76.
12 —Cf. Baia Curioni, p. 79.
13 —Giovanni had already contributed an article to this in 1849. Cf. Sartori, p. 44, 48.
14 —As quoted by Baia Curioni, p. 84.
15 —The correspondence on these negotiations can be found in the Archivio Storico Ricordi
16 —Cf. Baia Curioni, p. 143.
17 —Cf. Sartori, p. 67.

3

18 —Mosco Carner writes that the choice of pseudonym is "indicative of the growing popularity of German music since the 1870s" (Mosco Carner: *Puccini*, Frankfurt 1996, p. 103). The pseudonym's combination of a French first name and a German surname could also, however, be an expression of Giulio Ricordi's European orientation.
19 —Cf. Baia Curioni, p. 134.
20 —Cf. Sartori, p. 69.
21 —Carner, p. 104.
22 —Giulio Ricordi 1885 in the *Gazzetta Musicale di Milano*, as quoted by Baia Curioni, p. 169.
23 —Cf. Baia Curioni, p. 157/101 and 167.

4

24 —Sartori, p. 75
25 —Cf. Baia Curioni, pp. 202—204.
26 —Sartori, 76.
27 —Heinrich August Winkler: *Geschichte des Westens. Von den Anfängen in der Antike bis zum 20. Jahrhundert*, Munich 2009, vol. 1, p. 988.
28 —Cf. Sartori, p. 76.
29 —Cf. Baia Curioni, p. 198.
30 —Cf. ibid, p. 191.
31 —Cf. Sartori, p. 76.
32 —Baia Curioni presumes this, p. 198.
33 —Cf. Baia Curioni, p. 201.
34 —Ibid, p. 204.
35 —See Gabriele Dotto, "Publisher as Protagonist", in *That's Opera: 200 years of Italian Music*, Munich/Berlin/London/New York 2008, p. 21.
36 —Cf. the relevant passage in Baia Curioni, p. 205 et seq.
37 —Ricordi only published Mascagni's Iris (1898).
38 —All published by Ricordi.
39 —In conversation with his cousin Claudio, Nanni Ricordi says: "Tito II was a character I fortunately or unfortunately never met! He was someone who wanted the Giovinezza to be played before every opera performance." *Ti ricordi, Nanni? Con Nanni Ricordi, l'uomo che inventò i cantautori*, Milan 2010, p. 152.
40 —Cf. the comprehensive description by Maria Pia Ferraris, "Attività grafica di Ricordi", in: *Musica, musicisti, editoria: 175 anni di Casa Ricordi*, Milan 1983, p. 192 et seq.

5

41 —Cf. Matteo Mainardi: "Musica, Fascismo, editoria. Casa Ricordi tra rinnovamento e tradizione", in: *Editori e lettori. La produzione libraria in Italia nella prima metà del Novecento*. A cura di Luisa Finocchi e Ada Gigli Marchetti, Milan 2000, pp. 99—116, p. 100: "[Our] consultation of the 'Archivio storico di Casa Ricordi', where research was done on the correspondence with the state agencies (ministries), para-governmental agencies (associations and corporations) and Italy's major opera houses, above all the Teatro alla Scala, to which Casa Ricordi had always linked its fates, proved especially important." Fiamma Nicolodi and Harvey Sachs (Toscanini's biographer) also worked on this historical period.
42 —Mainardi cites the grotesque abridgements of the libretto to Verdi's *La Forza del Destino* (The Force of Destiny) 1936.
43 —Cf. Mainardi, p. 103. The letter in question, dated December 1, 1938, to the Ministero di Cultura Popolare is in the archive ("copialettere"). This letter is followed by several letters to the publishing company's authors, who are asked to indicate whether they are Jewish.
44 —Cf. Harvey Sachs, *Toscanini. Eine Biographie*, translated by Hans-Horst Henschen, Munich 1980, p. 292 et seq.
45 —Cf. Mainardi, p. 104.
46 —Cf. ibid.
47 —Cf. Mainardi, p. 105.
48 —Cf. Lamberto Trezzini/Angelo Curtolo: *Oltre le quinte. Idee, cultura e organizzazione del teatro musicale in Italia*, Venice 1983, p. 37 et seq.
49 —Cf. Mainardi, p. 110.
50 —Source: *Quaderni dell'I.R.TE.M. 14*, Serie 5: Cronologie. N. 1: *Le otto stagioni di Toscanini alla Scala 1921—1929*, di Carlo Marinelli Roscioni, Rome 1993.
51 —Cf. Mainardi, p. 111.
52 —Cf. ibid, p. 107.
53 —Cf. Sartori, p. 85.
54 —Mainardi, p. 114.
55 —Cf. Mainardi's remarks on this, p. 113 et seq.
56 —Cf. Sartori, p. 87.

6

57 —Cf. Sartori, p. 88.

7

58—*Ti ricordi, Nanni?*, p. 11.
59—Cf. Ricky Gianco's remarks in: *Ti ricordi, Nanni?*, p. 149.
60—Cf. Nanni's accounts of this in: *Ti ricordi, Nanni?*, pp. 156–157.
61—Giovanni Gavazzeni, in: *Ti ricordi, Nanni?*, p. 220.
62—Nanni Ricordi, in: *Ti ricordi, Nanni?*, p. 167.
63—"Nanni ha inventato i cantautori: questa gente che cantava per interpretare i propri canzoni." "Nanni invented the Cantautori: these people who sing in order to play their own songs." Enzo Jannacci, in: *Ti ricordi, Nanni?*, p. 130.
64—Cf. *Ti ricordi, Nanni?*, p. 169.
65—Mario Hyphenate, *Una vita di musica (un libro di ricordi). Catalogo delle opere.* A cura di James Westby. Introduzione di Mila de Santis. Cura editoriale di Ulla Casalini, Fiesole 2005, p. 147.
66—Cf. "La musica non morirà. Testimonianza di Luciana Abbado Pestalozza", in: *Milano, laboratorio musicale del Novecento – Scritti in onore di Luciana Pestalozza*, ed. by Oreste Bossini, Milan 2009, p. 34.
67—Cf. the correspondence in the archive of the International Music Institute in Darmstadt.
68—See the Collezione Digitale web portal launched in December 2016, http://digital.archivioricordi.com
69—An online edition of Giulio Ricordi's letters will soon be published, edited by Patricia Rebulla.
70—For instance, the performance of the opera *Tosca* as part of the "New York City Opera Renaissance" project in January 2016 was based on historical costume drawings and sketches from the Ricordi archive.
71—Bertelsmann SE & Co. KGaA press release, posted at www.bertelsmann.com/news-and-media/news/

**Founded as a company archive, during its 200-year history the Archivio Storico Ricordi has grown continuously, with changing focuses, principles of classification, and indexing structures.
As a historical collection with a heterogeneous structure, it also documents 200 years of human history: music, art, theater, cultural history, social and economic history, and political history.**

THE ARCHIVE

8

The Phenomenon of Opera

"Like never before and never since, musicians of the time were in a position to communicate with all levels of society."

LUCIO DALLA

The archive's diverse holdings and its research and information functions relate to contexts of music and cultural history, and the history of opera aesthetics. The archive contains invaluable material about the history of music, especially opera, which can be viewed as an artistic and social phenomenon. In 19th century Italy in particular, it takes on a distinctive mediation role in the socio-political structure.

The relationships between the great publishing personalities Giovanni, Tito I and Giulio Ricordi and "their" composers attest to how, during the course of the 19th century, the opera business changed from a theater-driven to a publisher-driven system. Both the historic periods and the linking of marketing and artistic concepts play a role in this connection. The diverse range of publishing correspondence documented in the archive illuminates this productive relationship. Not only is the correspondence with the "big five" – Rossini, Donizetti, Bellini, Verdi, Puccini – exemplary in this respect; the letters in their entirety shed a lot of light on this process of change, which also reflects a change with regard to how the works and their authors are perceived.

The appreciation of the original, unique works, and of the authorship of these works are new ideas in the opera business of the time, and the Ricordi publishing house plays a crucial role in this. In this respect, the archive is a rich source of clarification regarding the interaction between different societal forces of the time, as it documents the interconnectedness of artistic and economic aspects with letters, documentations of contracts, fee agreements, reception (eyewitness reports, reviews, correspondence) and marketing.

65—Cover of the periodical *Musica e Musicisti*, illustration by Franz Laskoff, 1902

Various search filters can be used to understand the genesis of the texts and music, and the performance history and reception of individual works. This also provides an unparalleled insight into the socio-economic fabric of 19th century Milan as an up-and-coming European metropolis.

The story of opera is fundamentally Italian, but also fundamentally European. At the time of the publishing house's establishment by Giovanni Ricordi, Donizetti- and Bellini-influenced bel canto opera still dominates the opera stage. The Napoleonic era is not over and the genre of opera is still bound to the ancien régime. At the same time the demands of the French Revolution and the beginnings of industrialization have also reached Italy, that politically fragmented region with the Regno delle Due Sicilie in the south, the Papal States in Rome, the free duchies in central Italy, Savoy in the northwest and the Austrian territories in the northeast. The goal of a unified Italian state is still distant, but the social and political movements against the privileges of the nobility exist. In a social climate affected by liberal and conservative forces, the musical landscape is also in a state of flux.

An old dispute about the primacy of music vs. lyrics in opera is settled by the bel canto opera in favor of "melody": Rossini, Donizetti and Bellini write incomparably beautiful cantabile tunes, which are spontaneously provided with additional flourishes during the singers' performance. The Archivio Storico Ricordi collection contains autographs of operas by these three composers, well restored and already digitized.

From the first decades of Giovanni Ricordi's activities, when he expanded his collection through

66–68

clever contracts so that in 1814 he was able to publish a first catalog, documents survive that testify to one of the secrets of the Ricordi company's success: the personal relationship between the publisher and his authors, whom he treats in a friendly manner. For instance, in a letter to Donizetti, Giovanni reports extensively on the success of a performance of the opera *Anna Bolena* in Paris — a success that he wants to tell the composer about immediately after his return as an eye witness ("testimonio oculare"), out of respect and appreciation for him.[72] Giovanni's European-influenced basic attitude, as shown in his various correspondences with publishers (Breitkopf & Härtel as well as Peters in Leipzig, and Boosey and Hawkes in London), and composers and librettists abroad, also contributes to the company's growing success. Using the international business language of the time, Giovanni corresponds in French with Boosey and Hawkes in London. The collection of "copialettere" begins in the 1830s: a copy of each letter sent from the house of Ricordi is archived — and in the early days, a "copy" was of course a transcript.

66—Vincenzo Bellini, lithograph
67—Gaetano Donizetti,
portrait by Roberto Focosi
68—Gioachino Rossini,
lithograph by F. Perrin,
circa 1850

69–71

69—*Le duc d'Albe* by Gaetano Donizetti, posthumous world premiere, Rome, Teatro Apollo, 1882 *Municipal square in Brussels,* Act I, set design by Carlo Ferrario, 1882

70—*La Cenerentola* by Gioachino Rossini, first printed edition of the vocal score

71—Receipt from Vincenzo Bellini for the sale to Giovanni Ricordi of the opera *La sonnambula*, January 12, 1832

LA CENERENTOLA

Melodramma in due Atti

Composta per il Teatro Valle, a Roma

DAL

Celebre Rossini

ed Eseguita da' Signori

Soprani	Cenerentola		Sig.a Righetti
	Clorinda	Figlie di D.n Magnifico	Sig.a Rossi
	Tisbe		Sig.a N.N.
Tenori	Ramiro Principe di Salerno		Sig.r Guglielmi
	Alidoro Filosofo		Sig.r N.N.
Bassi	Dandini Cameriere		Sig.r De Begnis
	D.n Magnifico Barone		Sig.r Fil.o Galli

La Scena si finge parte in un vecchio Palazzo di D.n Magnifico, e parte in un Casino di delizie del Principe

[illegible] C.R.Bild.8 Fr.30. MILANO e FIRENZE presso GIOVANNI RICORDI. Prop. dell'Editore.

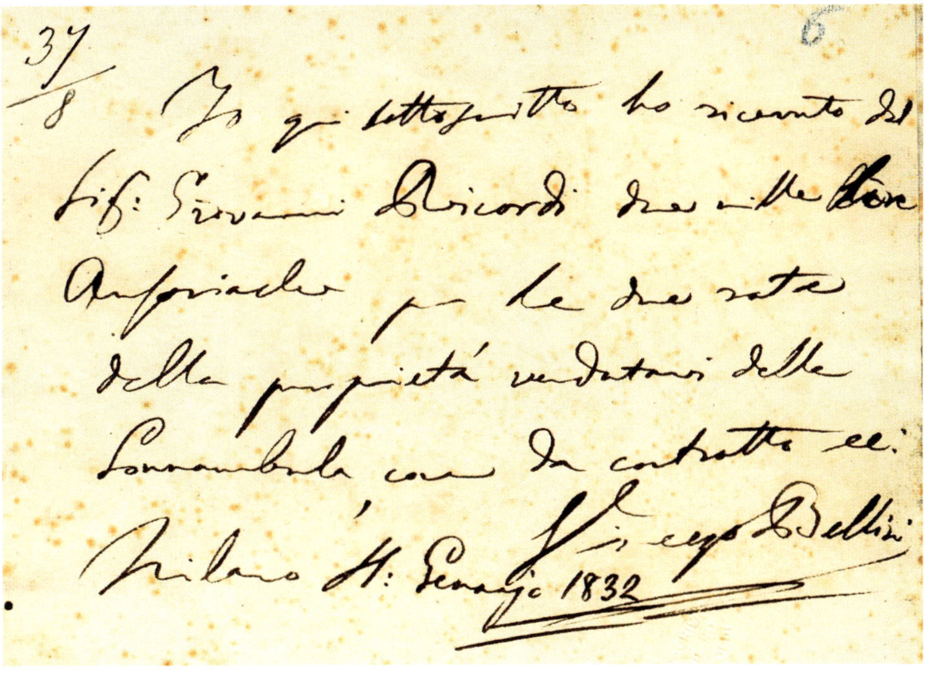

37/8 6

Io qui sottoscritto ho ricevuto dal Sig: Giovanni Ricordi due mille Lire Austriache per le due rate della proprietà vendutagli della Sonnambula come da contratto ec.

Milano 11: Gennajo 1832 Vincenzo Bellini

259
lento e sostenuto
19
Flauti 1 2
Ottavino
Oboi 1 2
Corno inglese
Clarini 1 2
Clarone
Fagotti 1 2
Corni 1 2
» 3 4
Trombe 1 2
Tromboni 1 2 3
Tuba
Timpani
(29)
piatto solo pppp
arpa
Mimi
Rodolfo
che ha detto il medico
Marcello
verrà
Musetta
mormorato
Madonna
benedetta fatela
Violini 1
» 2
Viole
Violoncelli
Contrabassi
61
senza sordini
tutti

The Collection of Autograph Scores

The heart of the archive, and certainly its most valuable part, is the extensive collection of manuscript scores — almost 8 000 of them. First and foremost, of course, are the "big five" (Rossini, Donizetti, Bellini, Verdi, Puccini). 23 of Verdi's 28 operas exist as autograph scores. Puccini's career is inextricably linked to the house of Ricordi, as all of his operas, except *La Rondine* (Monte Carlo, 1917), were published by Ricordi. (*La Rondine* was published by Sonzogno of Milan, the publisher of Pietro Mascagni's works. Conversely, only one opera by Mascagni, the popular success *Iris*, Rome 1898, was published by Ricordi.)

Besides these two important representatives of 19th- and early 20th-century opera, Saverio Mercadante, Simone Mayr, Franco Faccio, Francesco Cilea, Ildebrando Pizzetti, Franco Alfano and Riccardo Zandonai also deserve mention. A significant portion of the autograph scores has been carefully restored. The restoration has revealed deleted passages and amendments that have never been seen before, for instance on pasted-over pages that were not previously visible. The study of the autographs is fundamental for the reconstruction of authoritative editions and for better understanding of the compositional genesis of an opera; it can also provide an insight into the personality of the composer: the quality and texture of the paper, the type of ink, musical notation, and the manner of correcting, non-musical additions and dedications.

In the field of contemporary music, when forms of notation had become freer and more diverse, there are manuscripts by such great avant-garde artists as Luigi Nono, Franco Donatoni and Goffredo Petrassi. The younger generation is represented by Luca Lombardi, Salvatore Sciarrino, Luca Francesconi, Giorgio Battistelli, Fabio Nieder, Stefano Gervasoni and Fausto Romitelli.

The treasures of the autograph collection include the large archive of letters, which comprises, of course, the correspondence with Verdi and Puccini. Much of this has already been published, but the originals have a high commemorative and testimonial value. The approximately 15 000 letters contain extensive correspondence with composers, writers, librettists, singers, conductors, and other figures from the theater business. Indexing and studying these informative documents is one of the Archivio Storico Ricordi's most important tasks.

72–73

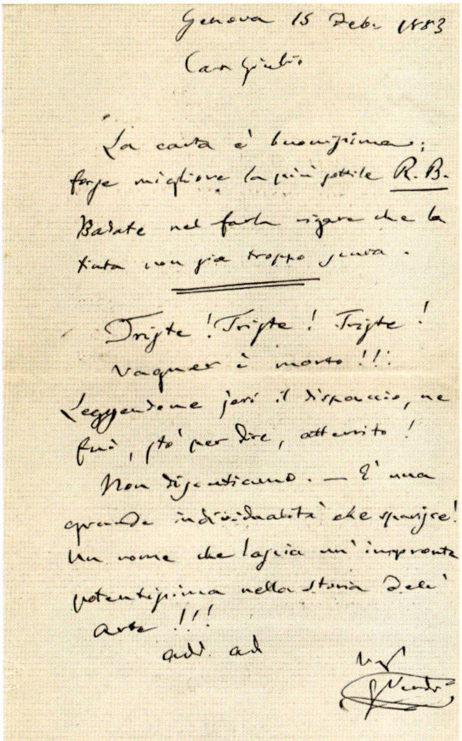
Genova 15 Febb. 1883
Caro Giulio
La carta è buonissima;
forse migliore la più sottile R.B.
Badate nel farla rigare che la
tinta non sia troppo scura.
Triste! Triste! Triste!
Vagner è morto!!!
Leggendone jeri il dispaccio, ne
fui, sto per dire, atterrito!
Non discutiamo. — È una
grande individualità che sparisce!
Un nome che lascia un'impronta
potentissima nella Storia dell'
arte!!!
Addio ad
G Verdi

72 —*La bohème* by Giacomo Puccini, autograph score, 1896

73 —Letter from Giuseppe Verdi to Giulio Ricordi: "Sad! Sad! Sad! Wagner is dead!!! [...] A name that leaves such a powerful mark upon the history of art!!!", February 15, 1883

74—76

74—*La sonnambula* by Vincenzo Bellini, autograph score, 1831

75—*Dixit Dominus* by Alessandro Scarlatti, autograph score, early 18th century

76—*Otello* by Giuseppe Verdi, autograph score, 1887

Otello
Atto 1°
Violini
Viole
Flauti
Ottavino
Oboè
Clarini
Trombe
Fagotti
Tromboni
Timpani
Cassio
Roderigo
Jago
Montano
Violoncelli
Contrabassi
Esterno del Castello
S'alza subito il sipario

1. a) Raragramma

a Romano
per il 4 agosto 1982

77–79

77—*Raragramma* by Sylvano Bussotti, autograph score, 1982

78—*Equale* by Stefano Gervasoni, autograph score, 1988

79—*24 Capricci per violino* by Niccolò Paganini, autograph score, 1817

con

…go 3ª e 4ª Corda

Important, but often Underestimated: the Libretto

The Archivio Storico Ricordi has an extensive collection of libretti, which Giovanni Ricordi begins to build early on, simultaneously with the music. Five groups can be discerned in the collection: manuscript libretti, typed libretti, printed libretti from the early 17th century, printed libretti that were not set to music, and drafts. Duplicates of printed libretti are often found, some of which served as the publisher's notebook during the performance and contain his observations about the staging and audience reactions.

Unlike the published review, this provides a direct eyewitness account of the performance history. The libretto, an object of discussion since the birth of opera, has repeatedly been evaluated differently over four centuries of opera history. Given the large inventory in the archive, there can really no longer be any doubt about the role of the libretto, though this does mark a convergence of mercantile and artistic factors: the acquisition of the rights to a libretto was often the first step in the production of an opera; not having a good libretto was a reason not to produce an opera. All his life Verdi searched for a good librettist for an opera based on *King Lear* by Shakespeare. The opera was never created: when, in his old age, he finally met a suitable librettist — Arrigo Boito — it was too late.

The ongoing indexing of the Archivio Storico Ricordi's important libretto collection, its cataloguing and structuring, provides an invaluable new resource for libretto research. This will result in new emphases regarding the preferred material and texts, but also regarding the development of the language of the libretto.

The multimedia presentation of various versions and editions of texts that illustrate the history of the libretto — complemented by examples from the correspondence — would give an insight into the origin of libretti, and thus into the development of the typology and poetics of the libretto as part of opera dramaturgy.

The archive's libretto collection dates back to the 17th century (items that predate the founding of the publishing house itself arrived in the archive through acquisitions of various publishers and printing firms, as well as the collections of impresarios). A thorough new cataloguing of this part of the collection is still underway. There are manuscript, typed and printed libretti, some with notes in the margin, little summaries, and some draft versions as well. One special item in the collection is a chronicle of performances of the *Stabat Mater* by Rossini in Bologna and Milan in April 1842, summarized in a small book. It is a collection of announcements, program flyers and handwritten notes by Giovanni Ricordi, a kind of "minutes" of the performances, but also notes about the money raised (these were benefit concerts for orphanages), the numbers of singers in the choir, and audience reactions.

The largest collection is that of printed libretti, because for each opera a copy of the premiere was preserved, then one edition each for other performances in other theaters, and abroad. The purchase of the archive of La Scala in 1825 enriched the libretto collection with rare items from the 17th and 18th centuries. There are also copies of libretti that contain entries made by the censorship authorities — moral and political censorship — from the time of the Risorgimento as well as the fascist period.

The libretti of Verdi's operas, for example, are subject to censorship in the years up to the unification of Italy in 1861. Censorship became heavier after the defeat of the revolutionary movements of 1848/49 in particular. But although political censorship was common, there could also be

80—Arrigo Boito and Giuseppe Verdi in the garden of Giulio Ricordi's residence in Via Borgonuovo, Milan, photograph by Achille Ferrario, 1892

80

considerable censorship due to moral or religious objections, which could vary from city to city, especially in the "Papal States" in the area around Rome. The archive documents various phases of censorship in its collection of libretti, letters and other documents. The affected works include *Un ballo in maschera* and also *La traviata*. The fact that opera no longer features nobles and heroes, but commoners (*Luisa Miller*), hunchbacks (*Rigoletto*) and courtesans *(Violetta Valéry)* on stage, and that political and domestic conflicts are dealt with, is new in any case. The libretto of *La traviata* ("The Wanton Woman") was a problem in 1853, before the unification of Italy, because it represents libertine views and gives them emotional justification. The various editions of the libretto in the archive demonstrate this clearly. There is an edition of 1853, which for the performance in Bologna includes the lines required by the censor. In the *brindisi* aria in the first act ("Libiamo, libiamo"), for example, the line "Croce e delizia al cor" (Cross and joy in the heart) is changed to "duolo e delizia al cor" (pain and pleasure ...) to prevent the connection of the metaphor of the crucifix with a courtesan. Another copy of the libretto contains the amendment of the word "croce" (cross) with "pena" (sorrow). A copy from 1860 is given the less scandalous neutral title *Violetta*, another changes the text of the aforementioned aria with regard to the motif of the intoxication of love and replaces the relevant passages with more harmless phrases related to alcohol consumption. The collection of *traviata* libretti is complemented by French, English, German and Czech editions.

Noteworthy among the autograph libretti are the libretto by Luigi Illica for Mascagni's opera *Iris*; the handwritten corrected version of the libretto of *Simon Boccanegra* by Verdi and Boito, which they both intensively revised as their first joint project in the 1870s; the drafts of the libretto of *La figlia di Jorio* with annotations by Gabriele D'Annunzio (music by Alberto Franchetti); and the libretto *I cavalieri di Ekebù* by Arturo Rossato (music by Franco Alfano) with annotations by the librettist and by Nobel Prize laureate Selma Lagerlöf based on the narrative of the text. In addition, the archive contains numerous contemporary libretti, some of which are drafts. The study of these sources enables a uniquely concentrated, meticulously accurate reconstruction of the genesis of libretti.

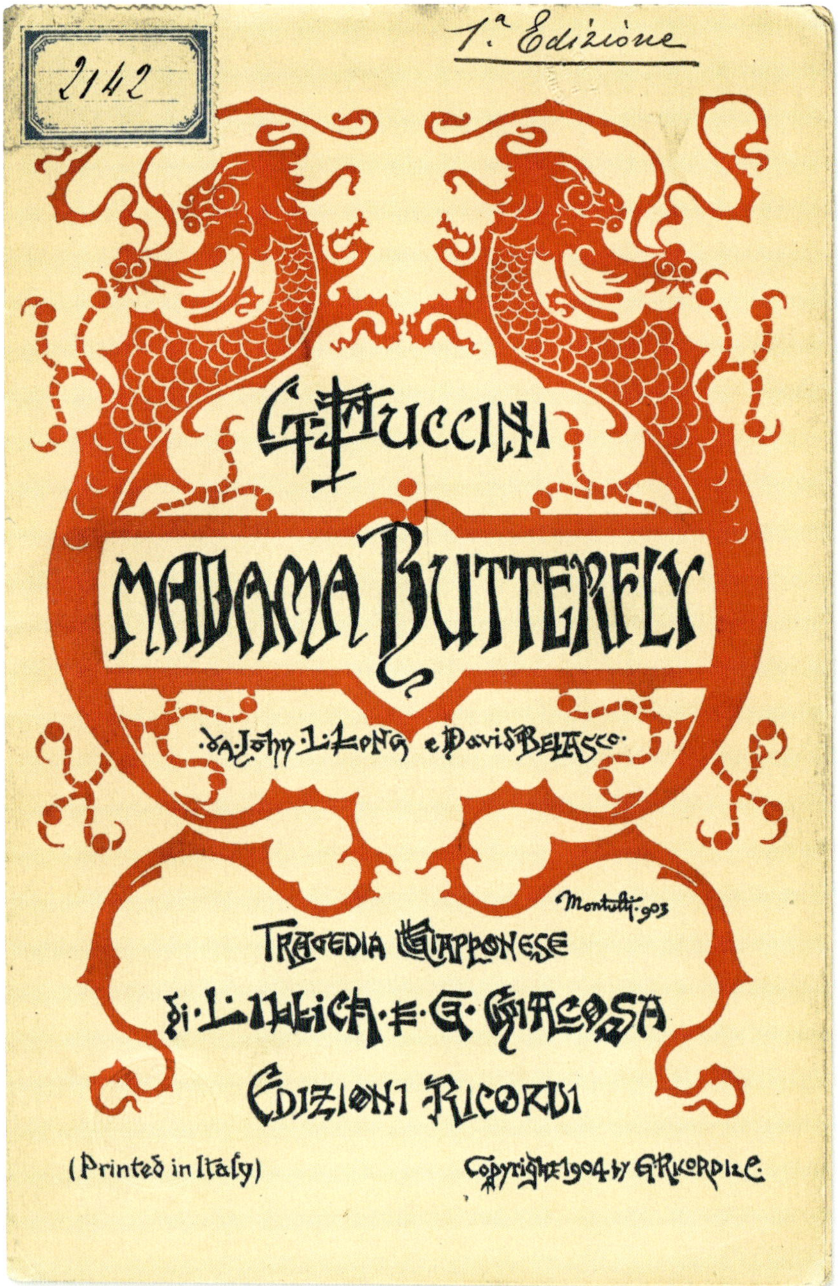

81–83

81—*Madama Butterfly* by Giacomo Puccini, libretto of the world premiere, Milan, Teatro alla Scala, 1904

82—*La traviata* by Giuseppe Verdi, printed libretto with interventions of the censors, proposing a new text for the *brindisi*, 1853

83—*Simon Boccanegra* by Giuseppe Verdi, printed libretto with annotations by Verdi and Arrigo Boito concerning the second version of the opera, 1881

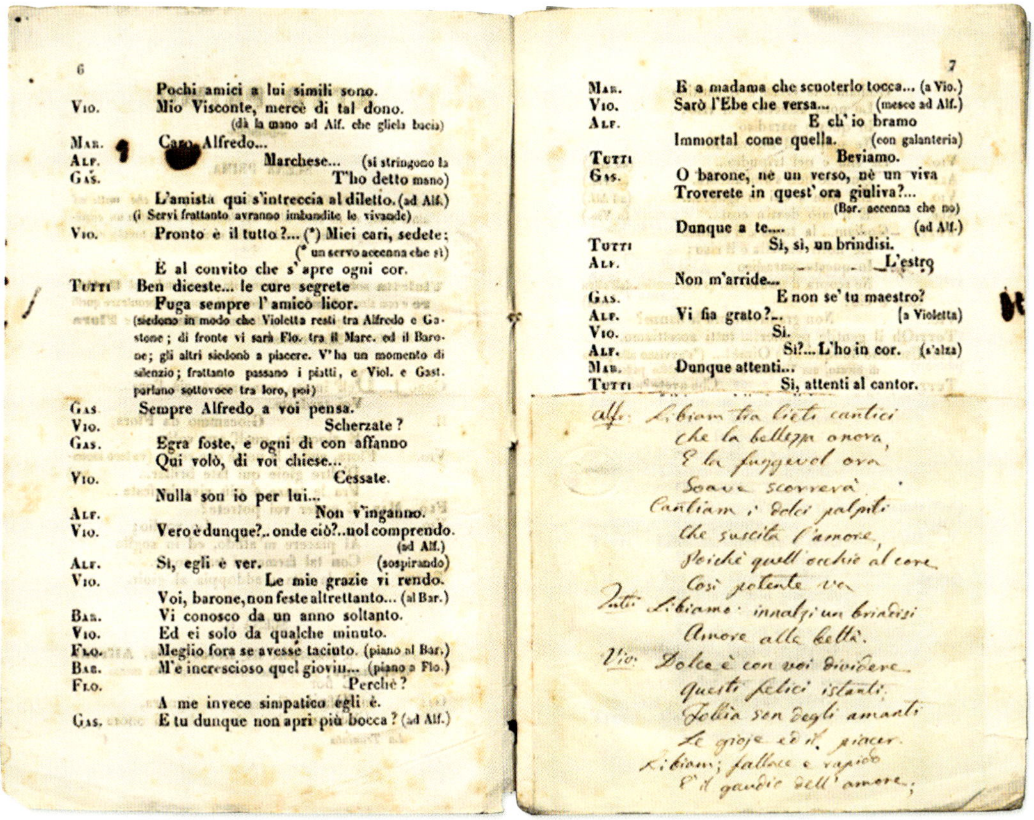

6

Pochi amici a lui simili sono.
VIO. Mio Visconte, mercè di tal dono.
(dà la mano ad Alf. che gliela bacia)
MAR. Caro Alfredo...
ALF. Marchese... (si stringono la
GAS. T'ho detto mano)
L'amistà qui s'intreccia al diletto. (ad Alf.)
(i Servi frattanto avranno imbandite le vivande)
VIO. Pronto è il tutto?... (*) Miei cari, sedete;
(* un servo accenna che sì)
È al convito che s'apre ogni cor.
TUTTI Ben diceste... le cure segrete
Fuga sempre l'amico licor.
(siedono in modo che Violetta resti tra Alfredo e Gastone; di fronte vi sarà Flo. tra il Marc. ed il Barone; gli altri siedono a piacere. V'ha un momento di silenzio; frattanto passano i piatti, e Viol. e Gast. parlano sottovoce tra loro, poi)
GAS. Sempre Alfredo a voi pensa.
VIO. Scherzate?
GAS. Egra foste, e ogni dì con affanno
Qui volò, di voi chiese...
VIO. Cessate.
Nulla son io per lui...
ALF. Non v'inganno.
VIO. Vero è dunque?.. onde ciò?..nol comprendo.
(ad Alf.)
ALF. Sì, egli è ver. (sospirando)
VIO. Le mie grazie vi rendo.
Voi, barone, non feste altrettanto... (al Bar.)
BAR. Vi conosco da un anno soltanto.
VIO. Ed ei solo da qualche minuto.
FLO. Meglio fora se avesse taciuto. (piano al Bar.)
BAR. M'è increscioso quel giovin... (piano a Flo.)
FLO. Perchè?
A me invece simpatico egli è.
GAS. E tu dunque non apri più bocca? (ad Alf.)

7

MAR. È a madama che scuoterlo tocca... (a Vio.)
VIO. Sarò l'Ebe che versa... (mesce ad Alf.)
ALF. E ch'io bramo
Immortal come quella. (con galanteria)
TUTTI Beviamo.
GAS. O barone, nè un verso, nè un viva
Troverete in quest'ora giuliva?...
(Bar. accenna che no)
Dunque a te.... (ad Alf.)
TUTTI Sì, sì, un brindisi.
ALF. L'estro
Non m'arride...
GAS. E non se' tu maestro?
ALF. Vi fia grato?... (a Violetta)
VIO. Sì.
ALF. Sì?... L'ho in cor. (s'alza)
MAR. Dunque attenti...
TUTTI Sì, attenti al cantor.

Alf. Libiam tra lieti cantici
che la bellezza onora,
E la fuggevol ora
Soave scorrerà.
Cantiam i dolci palpiti
che suscita l'amore,
Poichè quell'occhio al core
Così potente va.
Tutti Libiamo innalzi un brindisi
Amore alle beltà.
Vio. Dolce è con voi dividere
Questi felici istanti.
Follia son degli amanti
Le gioje ed il piacer.
Libiam; fallace e rapido
È il gaudio dell'amore;

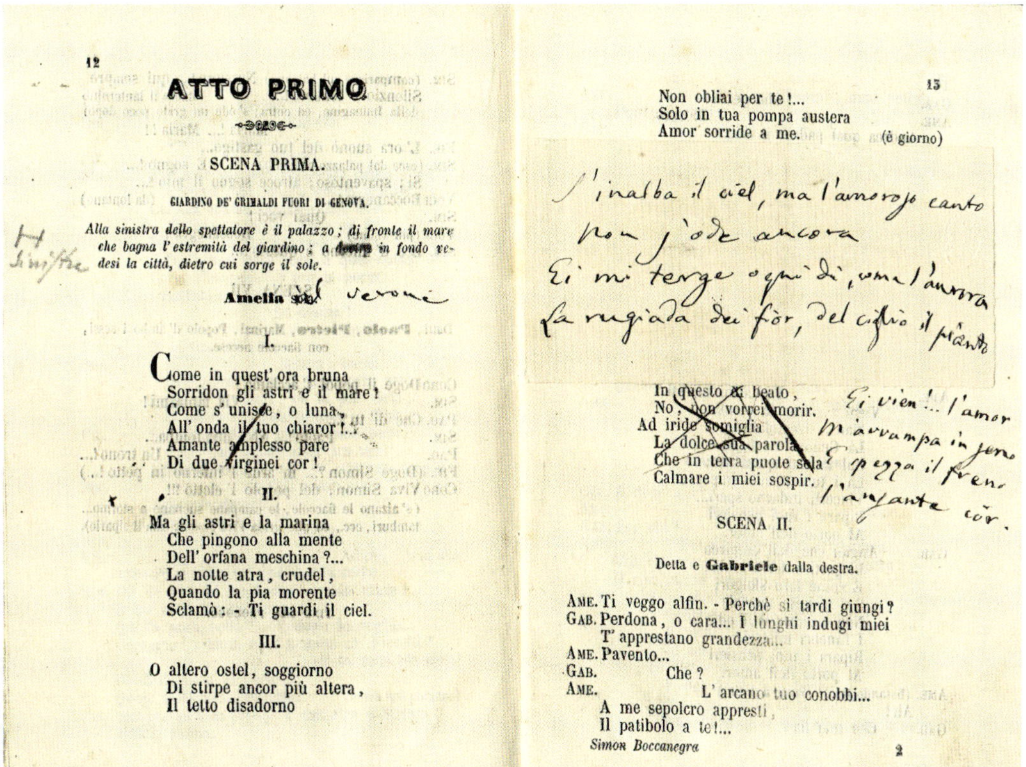

12

ATTO PRIMO

SCENA PRIMA.

GIARDINO DE' GRIMALDI FUORI DI GENOVA.

Alla sinistra dello spettatore è il palazzo; di fronte il mare che bagna l'estremità del giardino; a ~~destra~~ in fondo vedesi la città, dietro cui sorge il sole. sinistra

Amelia sul verone

I.

Come in quest'ora bruna
Sorridon gli astri e il mare!
Come s'unisce, o luna,
All'onda il tuo chiaror!...
Amante amplesso pare
Di due virginei cor!

II.

Ma gli astri e la marina
Che pingono alla mente
Dell'orfana meschina?...
La notte atra, crudel,
Quando la pia morente
Sclamò: - Ti guardi il ciel.

III.

O altero ostel, soggiorno
Di stirpe ancor più altera,
Il tetto disadorno

13

Non obliai per te!...
Solo in tua pompa austera
Amor sorride a me. (è giorno)

S'inalba il ciel, ma l'amoroso canto
non s'ode ancora
Ei mi terge ogni dì, come l'aurora
la rugiada dei fior, del ciglio il pianto

In questo di beato,
No, non vorrei morir.
Ad iride somiglia
La dolce sua parola
Che in terra puote sola
Calmare i miei sospir.

Ei vien!... l'amor
m'avvampa in seno
E spezza il freno
l'ansante cor.

SCENA II.

Detta e **Gabriele** dalla destra.

AME. Ti veggo alfin. - Perchè sì tardi giungi?
GAB. Perdona, o cara... I lunghi indugi miei
T'apprestano grandezza...
AME. Pavento...
GAB. Che?
AME. L'arcano tuo conobbi...
A me sepolcro appresti,
Il patibolo a te!...

Simon Boccanegra 2

Opera Production as Part of Cultural History

In the same way that the publisher rather than the theater represents the rights to a work, the production itself is also considered to be an asset worthy of protection. The figure of the "editore-impresario", the publisher as impresario, uniquely embodied by Giulio Ricordi, represents the publisher's job of monitoring the staging and the cast in addition to the rights to the music — and also, the expression of the desire for a kind of quality assurance for each production. From France comes the idea of "mise-en-scène", which Giulio Ricordi picks up and develops as "disposizioni sceniche" (production books).

Numerous original "disposizioni sceniche" are in the Archivio (some manuscript). In some cases, there are several volumes addressed to the various protagonists in opera production: the conductor ("maestro d'orchestra"), the dressmaker and the "direttore di scena" (the present-day stage director). The stage arrangements for the important opera *Mefistofele* (premiered 1868/revised 1875) by Arrigo Boito are divided into three volumes: Volume 1 is a complete edition for the "direttore di scena", Volume 2 is an edition for the dressmaker and prop manager, Volume 3 is an edition for the "maestri" (the conductors).

In addition, there are instructions for the singers, a glossary of theater terminology ("terminologia del teatro"), a list of props (three and a half pages), and, in a separate booklet, an illustrative overview of the props ("attrezzi"). The stage directions for the performance of *Mefistofele* at La Scala in 1881 were compiled by Giulio Ricordi himself in accordance with the composer's instructions. The stage directions describe every movement, every detail of the scenery and props, their position and use.

Sets and costumes are also part of the staging. The archive has a real treasure trove in this area. It preserves the designs and patterns for sets and costumes drawn up by many important artists such as Adolf Hohenstein, Alfredo Edel and Giuseppe Palanti, among others. The works show the meticulousness of the set designs of that time with regard to the historical and cultural context of the performances.

The same applies to the costume designs, of which the archive houses a vast and rich collection. The drawings of the costumes sometimes come with sewing patterns, samples of actual fabric patterns and instructions for the tailors. The impression of these unique pieces is hard to convey through digital reproduction; they must be seen, and perhaps held — the material has to be felt, or a pattern unfolded, to grasp the punctiliousness with which these things were made. A picture emerges of a time in which the individuality of each production is important in relation to the work. The archetype- and convention-bound world of the theater of the 17th and 18th century is supplanted here by a concept of theater that is individually tailored to each historical context. This represents the first step towards the director's theater.

Ricordi's efforts to achieve performances that are faithful to the work reflect an aesthetic of the "Gesamtkunstwerk" (synthesis of many individual pieces of art), which becomes popular in Italy as it is becoming popular in Germany with Wagner, and that requires a precisely controlled dramaturgy in all elements of musical theater: orchestra, singers, lyrics, stage design, and costumes.

Also noteworthy are the figurines for productions from the years 1902—1904 at La Scala in Milan, created by the painter Giuseppe Palanti (1881—1946), for *Un ballo in maschera, Rigoletto, Luisa Miller* by Verdi and *Madama*

Aida by Giuseppe Verdi, European premiere, Milan, Teatro alla Scala, 1872
84—*Radames meets Aida in the underground of the temple,* Act IV, scene II, drawing by Leopoldo Metlicovitz, Milan, 1902
85—*Dancing Priestesses,* Act I, costume design by Girolamo Magnani
86—*Mise-en-scène* by Giulio Ricordi for Aida by Giuseppe Verdi, edited by Giulio Ricordi, Milan
87—*Prop design n. 9* by Girolamo Magnani

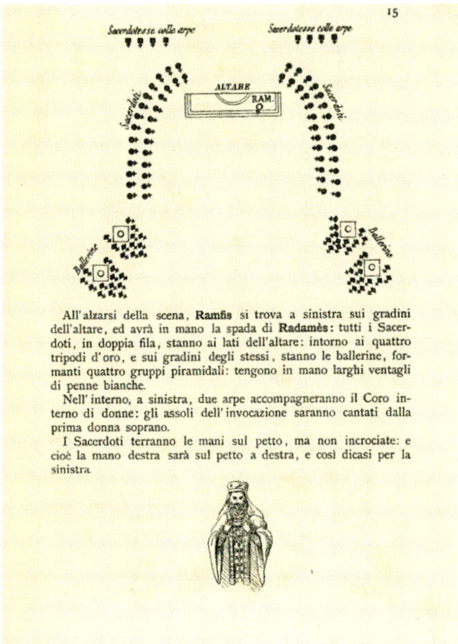
15

Sacerdotesse colle arpe

Sacerdotesse colle arpe

ALTARE

RAM.

Sacerdoti

Sacerdoti

Ballerine

Ballerine

All'alzarsi della scena, **Ramfis** si trova a sinistra sui gradini dell'altare, ed avrà in mano la spada di **Radamès**: tutti i Sacerdoti, in doppia fila, stanno ai lati dell'altare: intorno ai quattro tripodi d'oro, e sui gradini degli stessi, stanno le ballerine, formanti quattro gruppi piramidali: tengono in mano larghi ventagli di penne bianche.

Nell'interno, a sinistra, due arpe accompagneranno il Coro interno di donne: gli assoli dell'invocazione saranno cantati dalla prima donna soprano.

I Sacerdoti terranno le mani sul petto, ma non incrociate: e cioè la mano destra sarà sul petto a destra, e così dicasi per la sinistra.

84—87

Butterfly by Puccini. They not only reveal the equipment and design of each first performance of a given opera — the various examples also illustrate the history of stage aesthetics and director's theater. For the transformation of the opera in the early 20th century, which equally extended to publishing, theater, aesthetics and social significance, also had an impact on the monopoly of interpretation. The existence of opposing contemporary aesthetic tendencies — faith in technology, (self-)stylization and super-elevation of humanity, crisis of the modern subject, psychology and criticism of the idea of progress — also has an impact on the opera and its representations. The archive contains valuable material for researching these contexts.

88—90

88—*Madama Butterfly* by Giacomo Puccini, world premiere, Milan, Teatro alla Scala, 1904. *Butterfly*, Act I, costume design by Giuseppe Palanti

89—*Falstaff* by Giuseppe Verdi, world premiere, Milan, Teatro alla Scala, 1893 *Falstaff*, Acts I, II and III, costume design by Adolf Hohenstein

90—*La tempesta* by Felice Lattuada, world premiere, Milan, Teatro Dal Verme, 1922. *The King and Caliban*, costume design by Luigi Sapelli a.k.a. Caramba

il Re

Calibano

9

Verdi and Puccini

"The material in the archive is of interest to the whole world."

PIERLUIGI PETROBELLI

While Rossini, Bellini and Donizetti are initially the most important composers in Ricordi's portfolio, alongside such then-popular authors as Vaccaj and Mercadante, Giuseppe Verdi's entry into the opera world opens a new chapter in the history of opera and of the publisher, starting in 1839. The "Verdi era" extends beyond the time of Giovanni and Tito I up through the time of Giulio Ricordi, and is undoubtedly the most important part of the publishing company's history. The archive has autographs and libretti, letters, the costume and set designs of numerous premieres, and an almost complete documentation of signed contracts.

The story of the success of Verdi's early operas coincides with the history of Italian unification, the Risorgimento. There have been a vast amount of studies of this part of Europe's history of nation-building in the context of Verdi's operas, but the questions posed about the issues raised have not been conclusively clarified, and the study of the documents constantly sheds new light on apparently resolved problems.

For example, the famous prisoners' chorus "Va' pensiero, sulle ali dorate" — "Fly, thought, on golden wings" from *Nabucco* becomes a symbol of the oppression of the Italian people and for their attempts at unity, and during the "Cinque Giornate" in Milan, the uprising against Austrian domination, six years after the premiere of *Nabucco*, it becomes the "secret national anthem of Italy".[73] But the identificatory effect of Verdi's operas for the entire populace during the 19th century is not without controversy, and to some extent belongs to the realm of legend, as does Verdi's role in this.[74] The music of the opera was art music — only very rarely were opera melodies inspired by folk songs and, if so, usually to recall "couleur locale". Furthermore, folk songs were regionally rather than nationally influenced — as can still be seen in today's surviving Sicilian, Neapolitan and Sardinian folk traditions, to name just a few examples. However, the opera melodies were copied and played by "bande musicali" and sung and popularized through these channels. (The Ricordi catalogs of the late 19th and early 20th century offered a large quantity of "banda" repertory.) Goethe reports on this in his *Italian Journey,* but differentiates these experiences from the Italian "folk singing" that he requested the gondoliers to perform for him in Venice, and through which he learned the essence of the singing: "But this singing becomes human and true, the melody comes alive about whose dead letters we otherwise agonized."[75]

91—Giuseppe Verdi, photograph by Pietro Tempestini, 1899
92—Giacomo Puccini, photograph by Luigi Montabone, late 19th century

The boundaries between folk song and art music are admittedly blurred, and the importance of the "bande" is analogous to the importance of music performed at home in a developing civil society. So editions of traditional Italian "romances", as well as of opera scores for piano, singing and small ensembles formed an important part of Casa Ricordi's production. The archive has numerous printed editions, scores and piano scores of operas, and series like the *Biblioteca musicale popolare* document how Casa Ricordi promotes and caters to music-making in the home and popular interest in music. The archive allows for reconstructing the history of this area of music history, taking into account the music, lyrics, pictures, and correspondence.

The institution of opera itself in 19th-century Italy tends to be reserved for the wealthier sections of society. Most ordinary people cannot afford to visit the opera. There is a strict dress code and plenty of evidence that the opera houses only condone audiences from the upper middle class and

93—94

aristocracy. As late as the middle of the 19th century, 80 percent of people in Italy are still illiterate. In 1859 compulsory primary education is introduced through the "legge Casati", but in 1861 the illiteracy rate is still at 75 percent, and in 1901 at 50 percent,[76] although a certain difference between the urban and rural population must be made. One of the hindrances to literacy was the slow emergence of a unified or standard national language.

So the immediate effect of Verdi's operas during the Risorgimento concerns only a small elite. But towards the end of the 19th century, identification with Verdi spreads to broader sections of society — this is due to the popularity of Verdi's melodies, spread by the "bande", but, from the turn of the century, it also has something to do with the new replication media, the radio, the phonograph — and ultimately, with lower ticket prices in theaters. All this was not yet the case at the time of the Risorgimento. And yet, Verdi's operas *Nabucco* (1842), *I Lombardi alla prima Crociata* (1843), *Il corsaro* (1848), *La battaglia di Legnano* (1849) and *Un ballo in maschera* (1859) have become part of Italy's founding myth in the discourse about the Risorgimento.

93—*Aida* by Giuseppe Verdi, aria *Celeste Aida*, autograph score, 1872

94—*Gianni Schicchi* by Giacomo Puccini, aria *O mio babbino caro*, autograph score, 1918

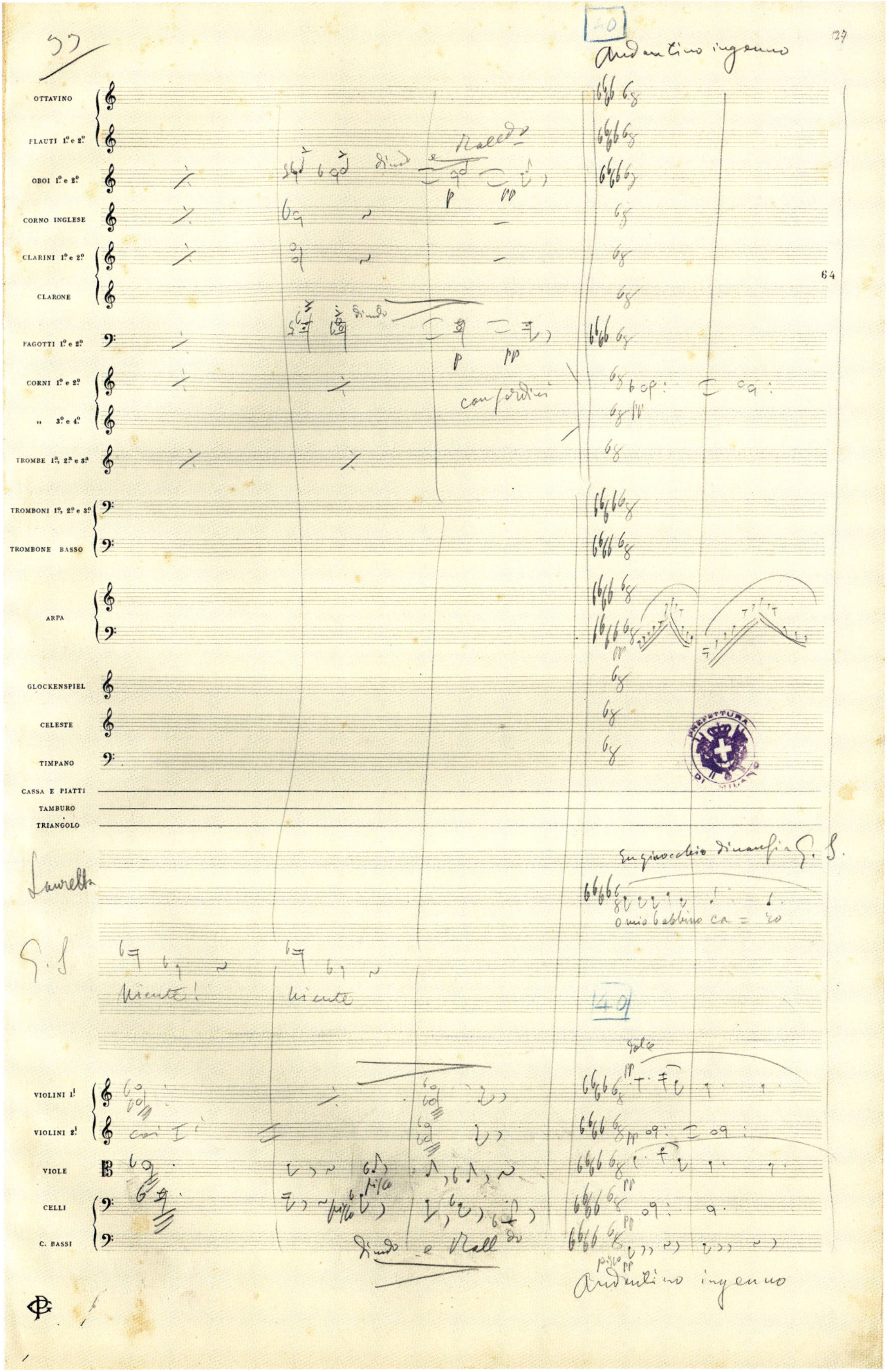
Andantino ingenuo
OTTAVINO
FLAUTI 1° e 2°
OBOI 1° e 2°
CORNO INGLESE
CLARINI 1° e 2°
CLARONE
FAGOTTI 1° e 2°
CORNI 1° e 2°
„ 3° e 4°
TROMBE 1ª, 2ª e 3ª
TROMBONI 1°, 2° e 3°
TROMBONE BASSO
ARPA
GLOCKENSPIEL
CELESTE
TIMPANO
CASSA E PIATTI
TAMBURO
TRIANGOLO
Lauretta
G. S.
O mio babbino caro
VIOLINI 1i
VIOLINI 2i
VIOLE
CELLI
C. BASSI
Andantino ingenuo

95–96

95—*Nabucodonosor* by Giuseppe Verdi, chorus *Va' pensiero*, autograph score, 1842

96—*Giovanna de Guzman [Les vêpres siciliennes]* by Giuseppe Verdi, title page of the vocal score, lithograph by Roberto Focosi

solo
cantabile
siero sull'ale do-rate va ti posa sui cli-vi sui colli ove olez-zano tepide e mol-li l'aure
190

Verdi's *Otello*

97

The success story of the Ricordi publishing house with the "blockbuster" Verdi continues after the unification of 1861. The archive documents the contracts entered into, the reprints, the single issues and the performances. After the first performance of *Aida* (1871), for 17 years Verdi cares less about composing and more about his country estate at Sant'Agata in Busseto, establishing a retirement home for musicians in Milan, the cultivation of friendships and contract negotiations for his operas. The collaboration with Arrigo Boito, the librettist and composer — a collaboration stimulated and guided by Giulio Ricordi — results in new impetus for Verdi's opera creation. In his youth, Boito belonged to the "Scapigliati" ("the Disheveled") artistic movement that broke with inherited tradition and developed new literary forms. Verdi always had a great admiration for Shakespeare's plays: indeed, he refers to the bard as "Papà Shakespeare".

Following on an idea proposed by Giulio Ricordi, Boito talked Verdi into the undertaking of *Otello*, an opera that is comprehensively documented in the archive, and is therefore a good example of the importance of the holdings for research. Verdi's enthusiasm for the material is authentic and mainly due to his love for Shakespeare. He repeatedly refers to the English text itself. His dispute with Boito over the libretto is documented in letters. Shakespeare's dramaturgy corresponds to what Verdi means by the concept of "inventare il vero" — "inventing the truth". The characters of Shakespeare's plays are for him "vero" in the sense of "verosimile" (translated as "probable" or "true"). He prefers the principle of "inventare il vero" to "copiare il vero".

Verdi's *Otello* can be extensively and vividly studied using the documents in the archive. It begins with the original contract between Verdi and Ricordi, dated December 17, 1888, witnessed by a Milanese notary called Giovanni Bertolè, which transfers the rights to the music and the libretto for a fee of 200 000 lire, graded by percentages and partial payouts. Attached to the agreement is a document in which Arrigo Boito transfers the rights to the libretto to Verdi for the relatively low fee of 4 000 lire. The autograph score can be studied on the screen as well, as there is a complete digital version available: but whether you look at it on the screen or in the original, what is striking is Verdi's austere-looking notation,

97—Giuseppe Verdi and Francesco Tamagno, who created the role of *Otello*, photograph by Pietro Tempestini, 1899

the rounded, closed, unobtrusive script and structure. A separate volume contains the ballet written for a planned performance at the Paris Opera, also the subject of correspondence between Giulio Ricordi and Verdi in May 1887. An introductory note to the autograph of the ballet shows Verdi's sense of dry wit: "Subito al principio all'attacco della tromba dovrebbe comparire un gruppo di Schiave turche che ballano svogliatamente e a malumore perché schiave ..." – "Immediately after the introduction of the trumpet, a group of Turkish slaves should appear, who should dance listlessly and without joy, because they are slaves ..." Some scores that were rented to theaters include conductors' amendments that were, at times, approved and adopted in later editions.

The archive contains different editions of the libretto for *Otello*. The copy that Giulio Ricordi took with him during the premiere of the opera at La Scala contains notes about the applause of the audience for each scene, and naturally, the bravura pieces are the most popular: the choir at the beginning of the first act, when Otello returns victorious – "Fuoco di gioia" (bonfires), Iago's "drinking song" in Act I during which he gets his competitor Cassio drunk, initiating the intrigue, the "oath scene" between Otello and Iago to avenge Desdemona's alleged deceit at the end of Act II, and Desdemona's "Ave Maria" in Act IV, which even includes a note that the piece was encored. At the end of the libretto text, Ricordi notes the exact order of curtain-calls. Furthermore, the archive preserves various foreign-language versions of the libretto in French, Czech, German and Portuguese.

Continuing with the documentation of *Otello*, we come next to the stage and costume designs for the premiere. The costumes were designed by the artist and illustrator Alfredo Edel (1856–1912), costume designer at La Scala from 1880 to 1890. The original watercolors are in the archive's holdings, as well as the figurines and the scenes. Who could possibly resist the charms of these unique documents?

The volumes of "disposizioni sceniche" (production books adopted from the French tradition of "mise-en-scène") are a special feature in regard to *Otello*. For *Otello* we see these "stage directions" in the archive for the premiere in a transcript by Giulio Ricordi. They go into minute detail about how to build and arrange the stage structures, what props are to be used, what movements the singers and choir execute, and the ensuing tableaus. Equally informative to the area of production history in this context are the "tavole di attrezzatura", plans for the props, which the archive contains for works including Puccini's *Madama Butterfly* (drawn by Giuseppe Pilanti) and *Turandot* (by Umberto Brunelleschi).

Similarly "complete" documentation can be compiled from the archive inventories for other important works of musical theater: for *Un ballo in maschera*, *Aida* and *Falstaff* by Verdi, *La bohème*, *Tosca* and *Madama Butterfly* by Puccini, for *Mefistofele* and *Nerone* by Boito, for *La leggenda di Sakùntala* by Franco Alfano and for *Iris* by Pietro Mascagni. In this way, the genesis and impact of the phenomenon of opera, between art and commerce, as a reflection of artistic and social developments, as a hybrid art form whose products are repeatedly reinterpreted and updated in modern opera houses, are clearly brought to life by the archived documents.

VERDI E L'OTELLO

Numero Unico
PUBBLICATO
dalla
ILLUSTRAZIONE ITALIANA
E
COMPILATO DA
Ugo Pesci ed Ad.º Ximenes

fratelli - **TREVES** - editori
Via Palermo 2
MILANO

Prezzo del presente Numero

98–100

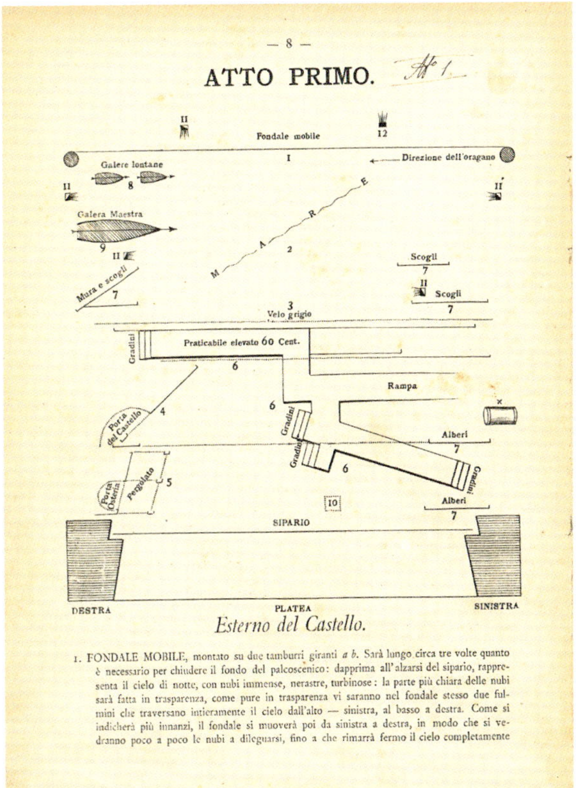

— 8 —

ATTO PRIMO.

Esterno del Castello.

1. FONDALE MOBILE, montato su due tamburri giranti *a b*. Sarà lungo circa tre volte quanto è necessario per chiudere il fondo del palcoscenico: dapprima all'alzarsi del sipario, rappresenta il cielo di notte, con nubi immense, nerastre, turbinose: la parte più chiara delle nubi sarà fatta in trasparenza, come pure in trasparenza vi saranno nel fondale stesso due fulmini che traversano intieramente il cielo dall'alto — sinistra, al basso a destra. Come si indicherà più innanzi, il fondale si muoverà poi da sinistra a destra, in modo che si vedranno poco a poco le nubi a dileguarsi, fino a che rimarrà fermo il cielo completamente

98—Special issue of the periodical *Illustrazione Italiana*, dedicated to the premiere of *Otello* by Giuseppe Verdi, 1887

99—*Otello* by Giuseppe Verdi, new production, Rome, Teatro Costanzi, 1887. *External view of the castle*, Act I, copy of a set design by Giovanni Zuccarelli

100—*Mise-en-scène* by Giulio Ricordi for *Otello* by Giuseppe Verdi

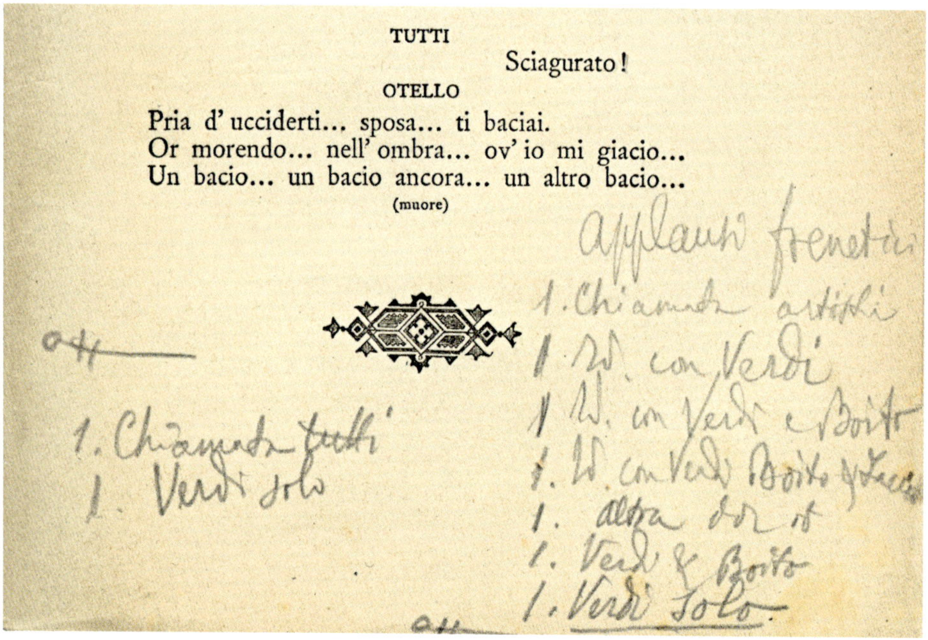

TUTTI

Sciagurato!

OTELLO

Pria d' ucciderti... sposa... ti baciai.
Or morendo... nell' ombra... ov' io mi giacio...
Un bacio... un bacio ancora... un altro bacio...

(muore)

101–105

101—*Otello* by Giuseppe Verdi, new production, Rome, Teatro Costanzi, 1887. *Desdemona's bedroom*, Act IV, copy of a set design by Giovanni Zuccarelli

102—Detail of the libretto with annotations by Giulio Ricordi about the audience's reactions at the premiere of *Otello* by Giuseppe Verdi, 1887

103—*Otello* by Giuseppe Verdi, world premiere, Milan, Teatro alla Scala, 1887. *Desdemona*, Act IV, costume design by Alfredo Edel

104—*Otello* by Giuseppe Verdi world premiere, Milan, Teatro alla Scala, 1887. *Chest in Desdemona's room*, Act IV, prop design by Carlo Ferrario

105—*Otello* by Giuseppe Verdi, new production, Rome, Teatro Costanzi, 1887. *The great castle room*, Act III, set design by Giovanni Zuccarelli

Desdemona

4

Sottabito di [illegible] bian[co]
quasi senza coda
Soprabito e maniche in
velo di seta e pizzo.
Grande ricchezza nelle
guarnizioni di pizzo e
perle — Borsa sciarpa
in broccato bianco e
argento, con cordoni
e fiocchi
N.B. Siccome la coda
lunghissima con la [illegible]
— [illegible] da [illegible]
quando si svesta.
Gioielli d'oro con pe[rle]
e turchesi.
Collana di perle
Gioielli di perle e tur[chesi]
da levarsi insieme alla
sciarpa [illegible] la
camicia

1° Soprano

Atto IV

Metri
Opera Otello. Scena 4.a

2.

di Desdemona.

Ferrario Car.

Al mio carissimo Sor Giulio
con affetto, il suo
Doge

Torre del La
4. Ottobre
'900

The Bertieri Platynotipe Studio — Turin (Italy) 25 Po Street.

Giacomo Puccini

Besides Verdi's operas, the operas of Giacomo Puccini are also all excellently documented: there are autographs of all operas (with the exception of *La Rondine*), all the libretti, stage designs, and figurines for the first performances of the operas *La bohème, Tosca, Manon Lescaut, Madama Butterfly* and *Turandot*. Noteworthy examples include the beautiful watercolor designs by Adolf Hohenstein, Ricordi's artistic director at the time, for the premiere of *La bohème* (1896 in Turin, conducted by Toscanini). Executed with great attention to detail, from Rodolfo and Mimì to the farmer's wife in the chorus and the gendarme extras, they not only depict the conditions under which opera was produced, but also represent the fashion and watercolor painting of the time. The same goes for the designs of Metlicovitz and Hohenstein for *Tosca* (1900), the opera that Mosco Carner has described as "a harbinger of modern musical theater."[77] In addition, there is an extensive collection of correspondence between Puccini and Giulio (as well as Tito II) Ricordi, documents about the reception the operas received, and photos.

The opera *La Fanciulla del West*, which premiered on December 10, 1910 in New York City, is a special case. Here again, the archive contains the complete set of materials. This is true initially for the autograph score and all printed editions. There are several copies of the libretto as well: with added descriptions of the characters, handwritten notes about the success of the premiere, and an accompanying clipping from a newspaper about a performance on December 27, 1910 in Chicago. There are English, Dutch and French versions, and various versions of the German edition by Alfred Brüggemann. The proof sheets of a printed score, used in rehearsals for the premiere, show changes by the hands of both Puccini and Toscanini.

As for the sets and costumes, Ricordi modeled them on the production of the play the opera is based on: *The Girl of the Golden West* by David Belasco in New York, 1905. Numerous photographs of this performance are preserved. A comparison of the stills with those of the opera premiere shows how closely the concept is modeled on the theater performance. The archive also contains comprehensive press reviews of *La Fanciulla del West*, including its foreign tours.

106–107

106—Giacomo Puccini, photograph with dedication to Giulio Ricordi, 1900

107—*Tosca* by Giacomo Puccini, world premiere, Rome, Teatro Costanzi, 1900. *Kiss between Tosca and Cavaradossi*, drawing by Leopoldo Metlicovitz

108—109

108—*Turandot* by Giacomo Puccini, new production, Rome, Teatro Costanzi, 1926. *Turandot*, costume design by Umberto Brunelleschi

109—*Madama Butterfly* by Giacomo Puccini, world premiere, Milan, Teatro alla Scala, 1904. *Three kimonos*, prop design by Giuseppe Palanti

BRUNELLESCHI

110—112

110—*Turandot* by Giacomo Puccini, new production in Rome, Teatro Costanzi, 1926. *Calaf,* costume design by Umberto Brunelleschi

111—Giacomo Puccini with the soprano Elsa Szamosi, on stage after a performance of *Madama Butterfly* in Budapest, 1906

112—Enrico Caruso, Pasquale Amato and Emma Kittlova Destinn, respectively in the roles of Dick Johnson, Minnie and Jack Rance in *Fanciulla del West* by Giacomo Puccini, Act III, New York, 1910

White
N.Y.
6

113—115

113—Final scene of the prose version of *The Girl of the Golden West* by David Belasco, 1905

114—Giacomo Puccini, *Manon Lescaut*, Act I: a page from the recently restored autograph score. The restoration revealed an earlier draft by Puccini, which he had pasted over with an amended composition, f. 104 v

115—*La bohème* by Giacomo Puccini, world premiere, Turin, Teatro Regio, 1896. *At the Latin Quarter*, Act II, set design by Adolf Hohenstein

poco Rall
oboi
Clarini
Corno inglese
Clarone
arpa
solo
poco Rall
Fagotti
Corni

CAFE

10

Searching for Clues in the Archive

"When I had questions, I called the archive and they always gave me the answers I was looking for. They have the sources there."

RICCARDO MUTI

One chapter in the history of music that is historically complex and has not yet been adequately researched is the period from 1938 to 1943. This applies especially to research on the work of Jewish composers, who were able to work in Italy relatively unmolested until 1938, but were then removed from the concert repertoire. At the Ricordi publishing house these include Aldo Finzi and Mario Castelnuovo-Tedesco, both of whom also wrote operas.

Aldo Finzi, born in 1897 in Milan, studies law at Pavia and composition at the Conservatorio S. Cecilia in Rome. When he is 24 years old, the Ricordi publishing house adds him to its program, and the 1956 catalog still includes his compositions: *Barque d'Or* (melody), *Cyrano de Bergerac* Bergerac (symphonic poem for orchestra), *L'Infinito* (symphonic poem for orchestra), and *Serenata: Stelle a notte serena* (by Longfellow).[78]

A comic opera entitled *La serenata al vento* was supposed to win a contest staged by La Scala for the 1938/39 season, and be performed that very season. But the announcement of the decision of the jury, which included Riccardo Pick-Mangiagalli (another Ricordi composer), is canceled at short notice, and the competition is annulled.[79] Following the introduction of racial laws in 1938, Finzi moves back to Turin and takes on translation and editing work under a different name. His compositions of the time went straight into the drawer: a symphonic poem that is later named after a Dante verse; a concerto for two pianos and orchestra, entitled *Danza*; an opera fragment *Shylock* (libretto by Arturo Rossato, who also wrote libretti for Franco Vittadini and Riccardo Zandonai); and a prelude and fugue for organ. A denunciation brings him and his family to the attention of the SS. To prevent his son from being discovered, Aldo Finzi voluntarily gives himself up, but escapes deportation by giving everything he owns to the corrupt SS. In 1944/45 he composes *Salmo*, a work for chorus and orchestra. Aldo Finzi dies on February 7, 1945.[80] Finzi's works published by Ricordi no longer exist in the archive, but an examination of the catalogs and business correspondence can shed light on his ties to Ricordi. A concert talk by the "Musica Reanimata" association in May 2012 at the Berlin Konzerthaus entitled "Masters of musical refinement" drew attention to Finzi. Finzi is acknowledged as a composer who, "at the age of 24 was already an author of the renowned music publisher Ricordi", who was "inspired by Debussy and Bartok, and then sought and found his own polystylistic path in the context of tonality".[81]

116—*L'ombra di Don Giovanni* by Franco Alfano, world premiere, Milan, Teatro alla Scala, 1914. *Vannina*, Act I, costume design by Pinchon

Mario Castelnuovo-Tedesco (1895–1968),[82] born in Tuscany, is a student of Pizzetti and a protégé of Casella and Malipiero. His diverse and extensive body of work is characterized by numerous works by Shakespeare — and also by other English poets, John Keats, Percy Bysshe Shelley, and later the American Walt Whitman — set to music (songs and operas), alongside compositions and songs for piano, chamber and symphonic music, much of it as yet unpublished.[83]

One of the leading composers of his generation in the 1930s, he is not among the avant-garde, but neither is he (like Alfano too, incidentally) a signatory of a "Manifesto of Italian musicians for the traditions of romantic art of the 19th century"[84] that is published in the *Corriere della Sera* in December 1932, an expression of the complicated discussion about modern music, intertwined with a debate about national traditions.

117—118

In August 1939, Castelnuovo-Tedesco first emigrates to New York and with the help of friendly musicians, including Toscanini, he soon establishes himself as a composer of film music among other things. From the mid-1950s, his compositions are restored to the Ricordi catalog via the New York branch. One important item in the archive, for example, is the autograph of the opera *Il mercante di Venezia* (The Merchant of Venice), which Castelnuovo-Tedesco wrote in 1956 and for which he won the Premio Davide Campari in 1958.

It only premieres at La Scala in 1961, delayed because Pizzetti of all people, who serves as consultant to La Scala, speaks out against the opera. Compositionally, Castelnuovo-Tedesco had moved away from his teacher Pizzetti, which may be a reason for this negative attitude. Even the intervention of Guido Valcarenghi, who was managing director of Ricordi at the time, does not help at first. Incidentally, the overture of the opera originated as early as 1932, and both overture and opera are dedicated to Arturo Toscanini, who was constant in his support of the composer until his death.[85] A detailed review of the correspondence in the archive materials and publications for the years 1920—1945 provides illuminating insights into the complex relationships between composers, librettists, publisher, theaters, and the institutions of the regime.

117—Mario Castelnuovo-Tedesco
118—Ildebrando Pizzetti at the entrance of the Teatro alla Scala, 1959

TEATRO ALLA SCALA
MARTEDI 5 MAGGIO 1959 - alle ore 21.15
PRIMA RAPPRESENTAZIONE
ASSASSINIO NELLA CATTEDRALE
THOMAS STEARNS ELIOT
ILDEBRANDO PIZZETTI
GIANANDREA GAVAZZENI
MARGHERITA WALLMANN
NICOLA BENOIS
NORBERTO MOLA
PIERO ZUFFI
PREZZI

H
La Principessa del sogno
BRUNELLESCHI

119—121

119—*Il carillon magico* by Riccardo Pick-Mangiagalli, world premiere, Milan, Teatro alla Scala, 1918 *The dream princess*, costume design by Umberto Brunelleschi

120—*Melenis* by Riccardo Zandonai, world premiere, Milan, Teatro Dal Verme, 1912. *Marcello suburban villa*, Act III, set design by Giuseppe Palanti

121—*Conchita* by Riccardo Zandonai, world premiere, Milan, Teatro Dal Verme, 1911. *Cigar sellers*, Act I, costume design by Giuseppe Palanti

11

Avant-garde Music

"I think it's wonderful if you stage Berio and Nino Nono … Evviva Italia"

WOLFGANG STEINECKE TO BRUNO MADERNA

The archive also reflects the development of contemporary classical music in Italy and beyond. It documents an important part of the history of European music after 1945. Starting in the 1960s, and seen from an international perspective, Italy is the source of decisive impetus for musical theater. Bruno Maderna, Luciano Berio, Luigi Nono, Franco Donatoni, Giacomo Manzoni, Luca Lombardi, Sylvano Bussotti, Salvatore Sciarrino, Giorgio Battistelli and many others represent very different aesthetic positions, from the politically motivated musical theater of Nono and Manzoni, to Luciano Berio and Salvatore Sciarrino's playing and experimenting with forms of memory and opera tradition, and the integration of electronics by Bruno Maderna, to new forms of ballet performance and installations by Sylvano Bussotti and Giorgio Battistelli, and literary opera by Luca Lombardi.

The increasing internationalization and expansion of the spectrum, and also the fact that the predominance of musical theater is being called into question in Italy as elsewhere, leads to instrumental music being published by Ricordi more and more on an equal footing. The archive inventory, with its large number of scores (especially autographs) of contemporary vocal and instrumental music, offers a panorama of Italian music from 1960 to 1990. Add to that libretti, correspondence, collections of reviews, and photos. The aforementioned composers are comprehensively represented in the archive with their works — an invaluable collection of illustrative material for individual and comparative studies in researching the musical history of the 20th century.

122—Luigi Nono

The scores of Sylvano Bussotti (born 1931) are not only an example of an innovative form of musical theater that works with elements of ballet and input from the aesthetics of performance, but also of new forms of notation and presentation: his compositions, often conceived as installations, such as *La passion selon Sade* (Mystère de chambre avec Tableaux vivants — roughly: Mystery with living tableaus) of 1965, *BUSSOTTIOPERABALLET* of 1973 and *Bergkristall* (Poema coreografico — choreographic poem) of 1987 are documented in the unusual autographs housed in the archive. Bussotti is a student of Dallapiccola, the great instigator and individualist, and at the invitation of Pierre Boulez and Heinz-Klaus Metzger, from the end of the 1950s begins staging his works at the Darmstadt Summer Courses. So the work of Bussotti documents both the international reach of Ricordi, and manifests the genre of opera as a "Gesamtkunstwerk" all over again, because his talents also lie in the field of painting, installation and choreography. Autographs, correspondence, photographs and reviews provide a comprehensive picture of this.

Many examples could be mentioned at this point, and special attention would be paid to each composer's selection of lyrics, for example Luca Lombardi's collaboration with Edoardo Sanguineti on *Nel tuo porto quiete. Un requiem italiano* (1985) and the opera *Faust* (1990), called "un travestimento", whose libretto was translated by Claus-Hobe Henneberg, the playwright and librettist, for the German performance. Collaborations like this between composer and librettist continue the tradition of the brilliant artistic connections, which spawned immortal masterpieces by Mozart—Da Ponte, Verdi—Boito and Strauss—Hofmannsthal, in a modern setting that is no less intellectually important than the historical contexts.

In Milan there is a special collaboration between the composer Luciano Chailly and Dino

Buzzati. Chailly, the father of the eminent conductor Riccardo Chailly is a student of Hindemith and one of the outstanding figures of modern music theater in Italy. Thanks to his aesthetic proximity to fantastical literature Buzzati, whose novel *Il deserto dei tartari* became world-famous, develops a kind of surrealist libretto, an appealing variation on opera literature. He wrote several libretti for Chailly: *Ferrovia sopraelevata* (Bergamo 1955), *Procedura penale* (Como 1959), *Il Mantello* (Florence, 1960), and *Era proibito* (Milan 1963).

Il Mantello, an anti-war piece, impressively portrays the pain of a family who have lost a son in the war. He appears as a kind of "zombie" to the waiting family with a bleeding wound under his coat. Buzzati does not give him any lines; he can only stammer incoherent vowels and consonants. This part is accordingly interpreted by Chailly as a speaking role: in the score he says the part is "tutta nugolata, vocalizzata, gutturalizzata, intozzata o belata" (whimpering, vocalizing, guttural, introverted, bleating). Chailly also uses double notes to indicate a vocal technique "come in un rantolo" (like a rattle). A review of the premiere (May 12, 1960, *Il Messaggero*) says Chailly creates a connection to the afterlife by using the "Ondes Martenot", a monophonic electronic instrument used from the 1930s by Milhaud, Messiaen and Varèse. In his review of the work, Massimo Mila highlights the "parlar cantando" that makes Chailly a master of dramatic recitation (May 29, 1960, *L'Espresso*). The Opera *Era proibito* has a theme that is critical of capitalism: in an office where employees are encouraged to work to a strict rhythm ("era proibito parlare, cantare, amare" — "it was forbidden to talk, sing, love"), the return of the moon (which was "forbidden" for ninety years) is surrealistically staged as an imaginary liberation. Among other things, Buzzati introduces a chorus of employees who imitate work onomatopoetically. The archive owns a draft of the libretto with amendments by Buzzati, proofs, as well as Chailly's autograph score.

The lively exchange between composers made possible by the Darmstadt International Summer Course and other new music festivals, together with other factors, probably also leads to Ricordi's increased internationalization. And so today the archive has numerous works by non-Italian composers, including Youngi Pagh-Paan, Gérard Grisey and Hans Werner Henze.

123—*Prometeo* by Luigi Nono, *I Isola (First Isle)*, heliographic proof for 1984 version with Nono's autograph annotation for the 1985 version

VLA
VC
CB
FL
CL
TR
TRB
PROMETEO
AURORA E TRAMONTO
ARCO MOBILE
A. MOBILE
SUONO COME SCRITTO
SENZA SORDINO

124—126

124—World premiere of *Prometeo* by Luigi Nono, Chiesa di San Lorenzo, Venice, 1984
125—Luciano and Riccardo Chailly
126—*Lorenzaccio* by Sylvano Bussotti, autograph score, 1972

(SC.)
incudine
incudine
2 a.
2 chit.
Pf.
Tutti battuti sulle casse con bacch. dure
sempre
vibr.
Pf.
secco
4 lastre
xil.
smorz!
smorz!

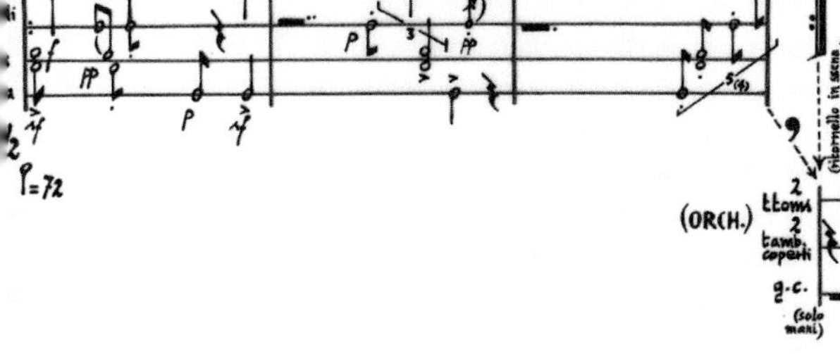
solo mani
tutto
estremamente secco!
staccatiss!

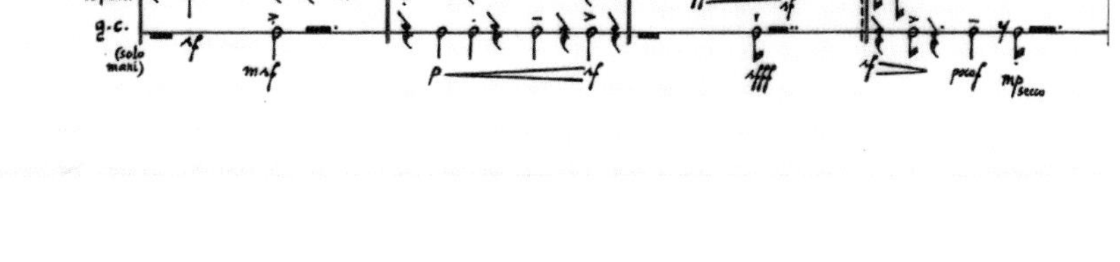
ritornello in scena sulle prime 3 misure
(ORCH.)
2 ttoms
2 tamb. coperti
g.c.
(solo mani)
ritenuto assai
secco

12

Reconstruction of Musical History

"[The archive] has all the information that will allow us to reconstruct the creative process that led to those scores."

LUCIANO BERIO

Opera is the dominant genre in 19th-century Italy. Only at the turn of the century do stronger trends towards instrumental music begin to emerge. The archive reflects these trends and offers ways to reconstruct musical aesthetic developments. In the period from 1912, Italian composers are also exploring the modern trends of atonal music and dodecaphony: Luigi Dallapiccola and Goffredo Petrassi. The "Ottanta" generation born in the 1880s, comprehensively represented at Ricordi, is more conservative and seeks to combine modern and traditional concepts: Franco Alfano, Alfredo Casella, Italo Montemezzi, Ildebrando Pizzetti, Gian Francesco Malipiero, Ottorino Respighi.

Franco Alfano is familiar to operagoers as the composer who completed the third act of the fairy tale opera *Turandot*, which Puccini left unfinished when he died. In his time Alfano himself was active and very popular as an opera composer. Much like Puccini, he has a penchant for exotic material, such as Indian stories. A case in point is the three-act opera *La leggenda di Sakùntala*, which premieres in 1921 at the Teatro Comunale in Bologna, is re-performed in Naples, Buenos Aires, at La Scala and in Dusseldorf and Antwerp, and is one of Alfano's most successful works. The archive contains extensive material on this.

Pizzetti's own approach to opera literature also represents an attempt at the renewal of the genre, as opposed to verismo. Casella toes a neoclassical line with a focus on chamber music, while Respighi, probably the best known of the group to date, develops great symphonic music with strong orchestral tones.

Finally, Malipiero is a very active artist with talents in many genres, both in chamber music and in works for big orchestras and the opera. His collaboration with Casa Ricordi well into the postwar period, his ambivalent position at the time of fascism, and his efforts to create new musical forms and ideas, which do not preclude sharp judgments about musicians of his time, are documented in an extensive collection of letters.

In Italy, the "Classical Modern" period from 1910 to 1930 can be regarded as a time of cautious searching for ways of renewing the tradition. The Archivio Storico offers extensive material for research on the subject. Publishing catalogs, bundles of individual letters, handwritten scores and the libretto collection provide information about a time in which various artistic movements thrive side by side, with varying importance. A history of the publishing company for these years has yet to be written — and should be based on the archive, because it documents the various forces acting on the musicians and the business correspondence in particular makes it possible to uncover and trace links between the institutions and people in a European context. The history of Malipiero's opera *La favola del figlio cambiato* (The Fable of the Transformed Son) by Pirandello is just one example of the interconnectedness between cultural policy and artistic development. Premiered at the State Theater in Braunschweig in early 1934, its Italian premiere in Rome is banned by Mussolini for ideological reasons, an action that has an impact on the development of modernist forms in Italy. Malipiero mentioned the ambivalent affair in a letter of 1946.[82] The archive keeps opening up new directions of research that lead back to the archive itself. Questions related to publishing policy can be followed up in the archive documents. What kind of relationship, for example, did the publisher have with the

127—*Turandot* by Giacomo Puccini, last autograph sketches, 1924

avant-garde composer Ferruccio Busoni, who repeatedly approached the Ricordi publishing house, and several of whose autographs are housed in the archive?[87]

The extensive collection of contract documents in the archive (which are indexed in a clear system), and the significant business correspondence, the aforementioned "copialettere", which is available from 1888 to 1962,[88] is relevant to these and other questions. Sorted by fiscal year, it contains copies of all outgoing correspondence. For each fiscal year there is an index of volumes listed in alphabetical order. This correspondence provides evidence of the lively publishing activity: correspondence with composers, theaters, set designers, costume designers, technical companies (manufacturers of paint, fabrics, paper, machinery), the press, institutions, offices, etc. A thorough research on this correspondence also shows how opera is designed as a "Gesamtkunstwerk" and market product from the late 19th century.

And so the correspondence with individual addressees can be filtered out over decades. A detailed study of this unique documentation provides insights into the development of contracts with the authors, as well as with opera houses; about the

128—129

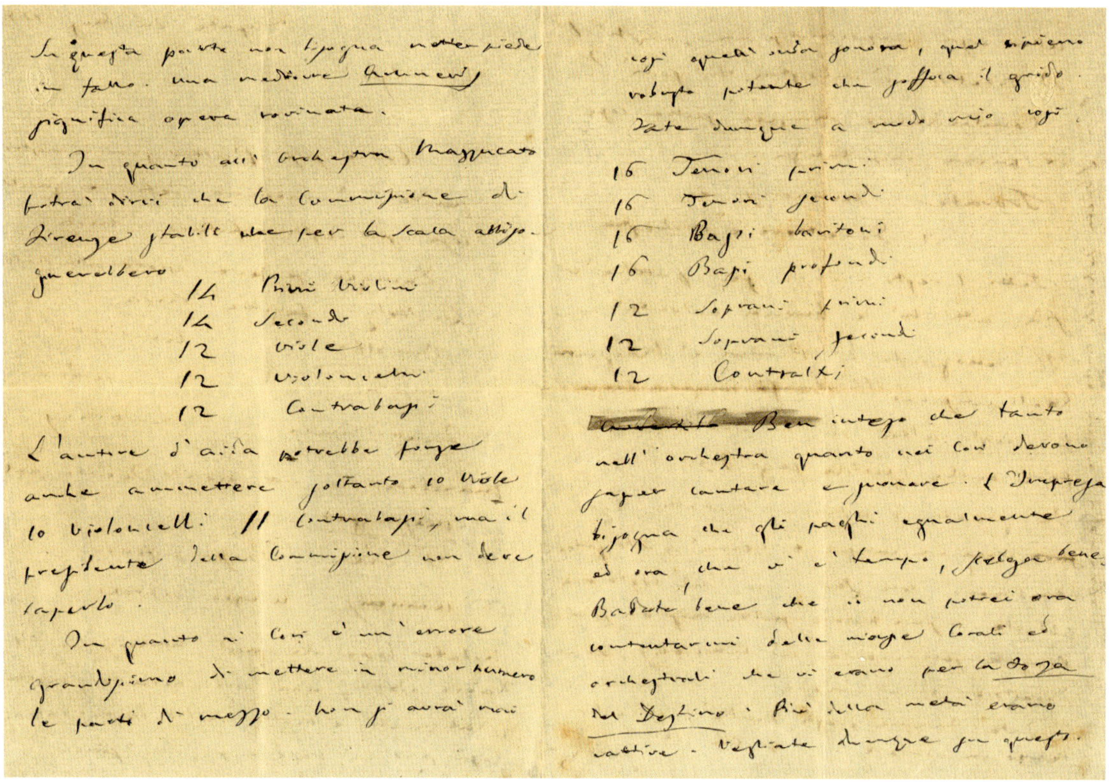
14 Primi Violini
14 Secondi
12 Viole
12 Violoncelli
12 Contrabassi

16 Tenori primi
16 Tenori secondi
16 Bassi baritoni
16 Bassi profondi
12 Soprani primi
12 Soprani secondi
12 Contralti

purchase of new presses, paints and paper; about negotiations of rights issues; about the addition of new writers; press contacts, concert agencies and much more. For instance, contracts may even cover the production conditions. From Verdi's correspondence, we know how this area becomes more and more important: which singers, orchestra, cast members and conductors are hired and much more. The stage arrangements are also part of this.

During the postwar period, Italy's intellectual circles are gripped by a liberating mood of renewal. The years 1943 to 1945, the years of the Resistenza, lead to a high level of politicization, which lingers on into the postwar period. The theses of Antonio Gramsci, one of the founders of the Italian Communist Party, regarding the educationally important role of culture and art on the whole of society become influential for writers, painters and musicians. In this context, the arts — including music — are not marked by a desire for depoliticized, purely abstract music, and they are not afraid to pick up on tradition: the lyrical cantabile in the field of singing; the aesthetics of polytonality and atonality, and twelve-tone composition, cultivated during the classic modern period of the 1920s and 1930s in Italy as elsewhere; and in the field of opera, forms of literary opera.

Ricordi's publishing program reflects these different trends. As a result of diversification in the musical landscape, the changes in society, and not least the changes to the publishing company's structure, the archive no longer presents such a complete picture of these years as it does for the years of Verdi and Puccini. It's been a long time since there were dominant individual personalities, and the music industry itself now has to contend with competition in the genre of film, and also increasingly with television. The separation of classical and popular music is now permanent, and the boom in popular music is unprecedented. Interest in sheet music in the field of traditional ballads, songs and extracts from operas continues, as evidenced in the catalogs from those years.

128—Letter from Giuseppe Verdi to Giulio Ricordi, Sant'Agata, May 24, 1871

129—Francis Poulenc and Goffredo Petrassi at Villa d'Este in Cernobbio, jury members of a competition sponsored by Casa Ricordi, 1958

FALSTAFF
DI
G.VERDI
ATTO PRIMO - PARTE PRIMA
L'INTERNO DELL'OSTERIA DELLA GIARRETTIERA.
ALLEGRO VIVACE ♩= 116
(s'alza il sipario)
FLAUTI
OTTAVINO
OBOI
CLARINETTI in DO
FAGOTTI
CORNI in MI
CORNI in DO
TRE TROMBE in DO
TRE TROMBONI
TROMBONE BASSO
TIMPANI
GRAN CASSA
DR CAJUS
BARDOLFO
FALSTAFF
PISTOLA
VIOLINI
VIOLE
VIOLONCELLI
CONTRABBASSI
Proprietà G. RICORDI & C. Editori-Stampatori, MILANO.
Tutti i diritti sono riservati.
Copyright 1893, by G. Ricordi & Co.
96180

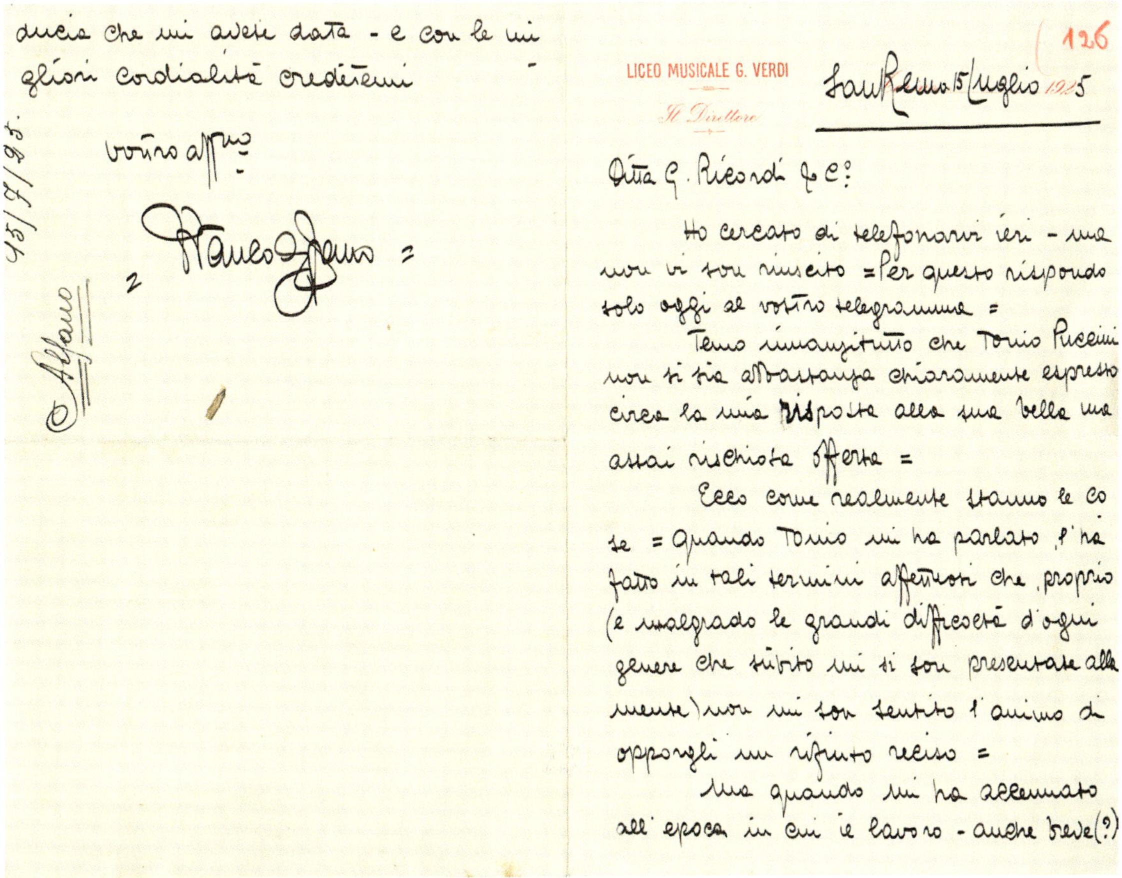

126

LICEO MUSICALE G. VERDI
Il Direttore

San Remo 15 Luglio 1925

Ditta G. Ricordi & C.°

Ho cercato di telefonarvi ieri - ma non vi son riuscito = Per questo rispondo solo oggi al vostro telegramma =

Temo innanzitutto che Tonio Puccini non si sia abbastanza chiaramente espresso circa la mia risposta alla sua bella ma assai rischiosa offerta =

Ecco come realmente stanno le cose = Quando Tonio mi ha parlato, l'ha fatto in tali termini affettuosi che, proprio (e malgrado le grandi difficoltà d'ogni genere che subito mi si son presentate alla mente) non mi son sentito l'animo di opporgli un rifiuto reciso =

Ma quando mi ha accennato all'epoca in cui il lavoro - anche breve(?)

ducia che mi avete data - e con le migliori cordialità credetemi

vostro aff.mo

= Franco Alfano =

15/7/25

Alfano

130—132

130—*Falstaff* by Giuseppe Verdi, engraved plate used as matrix for the printed score, 1893

131—Letter from Franco Alfano to Casa Ricordi, San Remo, July 15, 1925

132—Ferruccio Busoni with his dog, early 20th century

133—135

133—Antonio Puccini, Tito II Ricordi and Giacomo Puccini, early 20th century
134—Giacomo Puccini with his wife Elvira and son Antonio, in the garden of his villa at Torre del Lago, early 20th century
135—*Concerto per orchestra Op. 61* by Alfredo Casella, autograph score, 1937

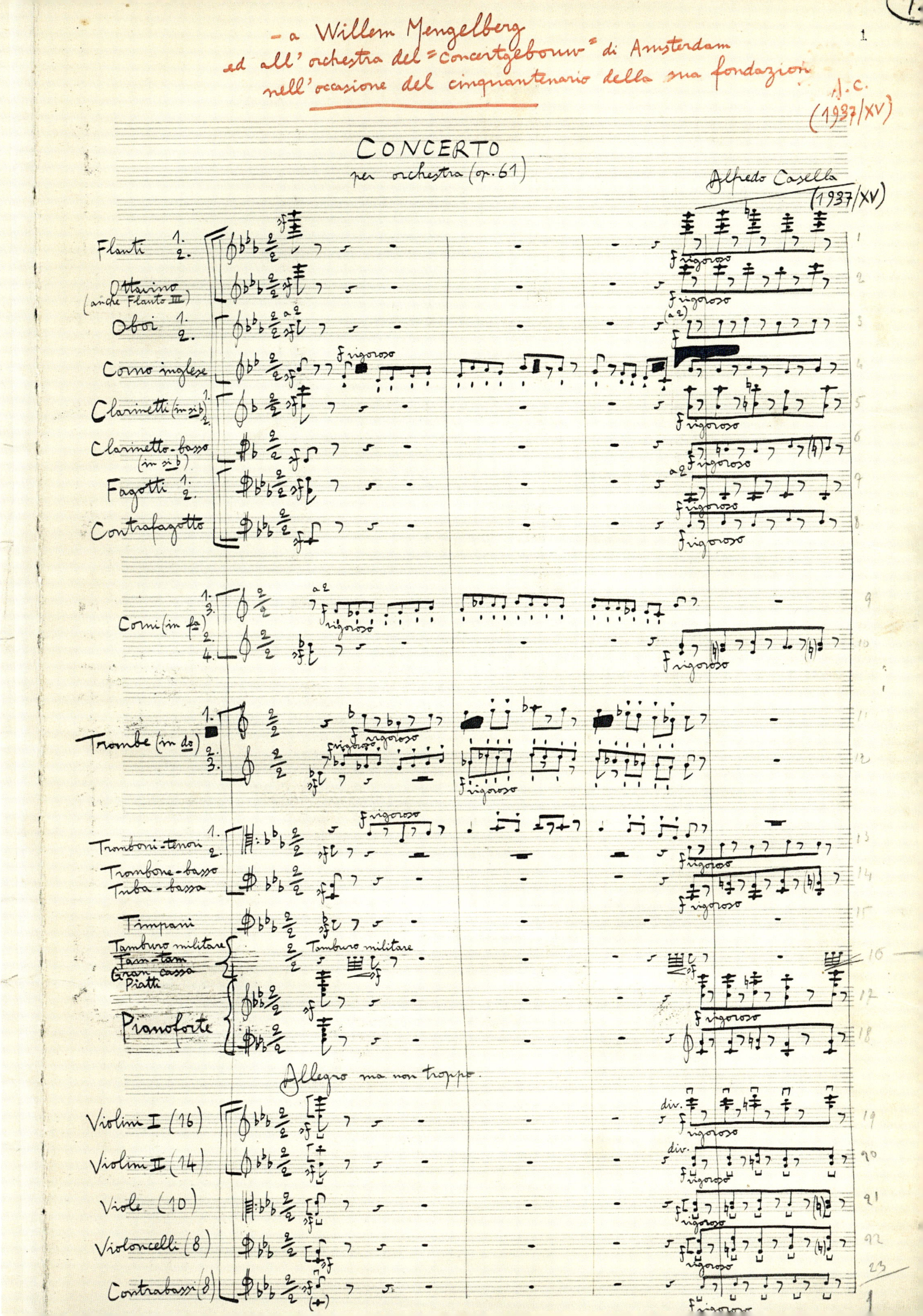

– a Willem Mengelberg
ed all'orchestra del "Concertgebouw" di Amsterdam
nell'occasione del cinquantenario della sua fondazione
A.C.
(1937/XV)
1
CONCERTO
per orchestra (op. 61)
Alfredo Casella
(1937/XV)
Flauti 1. 2.
Ottavino (anche Flauto III)
Oboi 1. 2.
Corno inglese
Clarinetti (in si♭) 1. 2.
Clarinetto-basso (in si♭)
Fagotti 1. 2.
Contrafagotto
Corni (in fa) 1. 3. 2. 4.
Trombe (in do) 1. 2. 3.
Tromboni-tenori 1. 2.
Trombone-basso
Tuba-bassa
Timpani
Tamburo militare
Tam-tam
Gran cassa
Piatti
Pianoforte
Allegro ma non troppo
Violini I (16)
Violini II (14)
Viole (10)
Violoncelli (8)
Contrabassi (8)
f rigoroso
div.

Outlook

In its entirety, the Archivio Storico Ricordi represents 200 years of cultural history, as reflected in the history of a company. The original company archives, which primarily served a commercial purpose, have become a historical archive. This process occurs at a time when European culture, which undoubtedly includes the tradition of opera represented by Ricordi, faces great challenges and the preservation of its heritage is becoming a priority in cultural policy. Many questions arising from the long history of the Ricordi publishing house are still relevant today: The compatibility of art and business, say, of creativity and entrepreneurship; terms that are not a contradiction in this unique company history.

Bertelsmann, itself founded as a publishing house in 1835, is well aware of the responsibility that such a valuable cultural legacy entails. Not only the history itself, but also how one deals with it are of great relevance in the context of the global (media) economy. So, what goals to aim for?

With the aspiration of making it a local and international best-practice case for communicating the content of cultural-historical archives in the digital age, the Archivio Ricordi has been systematically indexed and digitized since 2011. All the activities of Ricordi & Co., which is the legal entity behind the Archivio, are focused on safeguarding, preserving, and indexing the archive's inventory, and making it accessible. International exhibitions in Berlin (2013), Brussels (2013) and Madrid (2016), as well as collaborations such as with the Teatro alla Scala in Milan (2016) and the Victoria & Albert Museum in London (2017), have significantly raised its visibility and generated positive feedback everywhere. In addition, after several years of preparation, the Collezione Digitale online platform, which makes thousands of documents from Italian operatic history digitally accessible and searchable, went online at the end of 2016. Other ongoing projects and partnerships are aimed at the digital publication of individual inventories, but also at presenting the archive in the context of current performances and new productions.[89]

Bertelsmann is pursuing a clear objective with this: Preserving the Archivio Storico Ricordi only makes sense if its inventories can be successfully embedded in a contemporary context, and can serve to renew our perspective on the past. And so this remarkable project reflects back on today's company and is an important element in Bertelsmann's international cultural commitment, in which all initiatives are closely related to the content, corporate history and cultural impact of its products. In this way, Bertelsmann can combine its own publishing tradition with the requirements of handling our cultural heritage in the digital age.

136—Exhibition "The Enterprise of Opera—Verdi. Boito. Ricordi."; Gütersloh, 2013. The exhibition of original documents from the archive was shown in Berlin, Gütersloh and Milan to mark Verdi Year 2013, and attracted thousands of visitors.

137—Exhibition "The Making of Verdi's '*Otello*' — A Glimpse into the Archivio Storico Ricordi" at Madrid's Teatro Real to accompany the opening of the opera season with Verdi's *Otello* for the opera house's bicentennial, September 2016

136—137

Footnotes

8

72—Copialettere, 1831.

9

73—Peter Kammerer, quoted by Birgit Pauls: *Giuseppe Verdi und das Risorgimento. Ein politischer Mythos im Prozeß der Nationenbildung*, Berlin 1996, p. 182.

74—See in this regard Roger Parker, *"Arpa d'or dei fatidici vati": The Verdian patriotic chorus in the 1840s*, Parma 1997.

75—Johann Wolfgang Goethe, *Italienische Reise*, Frankfurt am Main 1976, p. 113.

76—Cf. Immacolata Amodeo: *Das Opernhafte. Eine Studie zum "gusto melodrammatico" in Italien und Europa*, Bielefeld 2007, p. 119.

77—Carner, p. 612.

10

78—According to the Aldo Finzi Society the work was created in 1933; Eleonora Carapella gives 1934 as the year it was performed and 1935 for the edition. Eleonora Carapella: "Musicisti ebrei nell'Italia delle persecuzioni: il caso Aldo Finzi", http://www.aldo-finzi.com, p. 27.

79—Cf. Carapella, pp. 6–7. *La Serenata al vento* was first performed on December 1, 2012 at the Teatro Donizetti in Bergamo as part of the Bergamo Musica Festival.

80—Comprehensive list of works by Carapella, pp. 27–29.

81—Georg Beck in "Musikforum", Deutschlandradio, September 24, 2012.

82—The Castelnuovo and Finzi families were related. Cf. Castelnuovo-Tedesco, p. 50.

83—Cf. The catalog of works *Catalogo delle opere* published by James Westby, Fiesole 2005.

84—"Manifesto di Musicisti italiani per la tradizione dell'arte romantica dell'800". Signed by Respighi, Casella and Malipiero among others.

85—Cf. the memoirs of Castelnuovo-Tedesco, p. 595.

12

86—"Ella deve ricordare che le preoccupazioni di casa Ricordi, nei miei riguardi, sono sempre state provocate dalla mia difficile posizione di fronte alla musica fascista. Ricorderà gli incidenti della 'favola del figlio cambiato', e le conseguenze dell'essere caduto in disgrazia per non essendo stato mai 'in grazia'." — "You should recall that Casa Ricordi's concern about me was always engendered by my difficult position towards fascist music. You will recall the incidents surrounding the 'story of the switched son' and the results of falling into disgrace without ever having been in a state of 'grace'." (Letter dated May 29, 1946, Archivio Storico Ricordi)

87—For Busoni's correspondence with Casa Ricordi cf. Fiamma Nicolodi: Gusti e tendenze del Novecento musicale in Italia, Florence 1982, p. 231

88—Also, some sporadic indexes exist from 1831.

89—For example, Bertelsmann supported the Berlin premiere of Verdi's opera *Stiffelio* at the Konzerthaus in Berlin, performed by Berliner Operngruppe on February 1, 2017.

138—The Archivio Storico Ricordi
today

7 800 Handwritten Scores
31 000 Letters
10 000 Libretti
13 500 Iconographic Designs
6 000 Photographs
Hundreds of Periodicals
Thousands of Printed Scores
Complete Business Correspondence
from 1888 to 1962

OVERVIEW OF THE COLLECTIONS

Handwritten Scores

Almost 8 000 scores from the mid-1700s to the end of the 20th century — not just opera, but also chamber music and symphonic music. The oldest are *Il Ciro riconosciuto* by Niccolò Jommelli of 1744 and *24 Capricci* by Niccolò Paganini; among the most recent are scores by Luigi Nono (e. g. his major work of musical theater *Prometeo*, 1984) and Franco Donatoni (e. g. his arrangement of Bach's *Kunst der Fuge* for orchestra, 1992). There are also a large number of "romances" that are still performed in Italy today, by Francesco Paolo Tosti and others, arrangements, and a range of works for musical education.

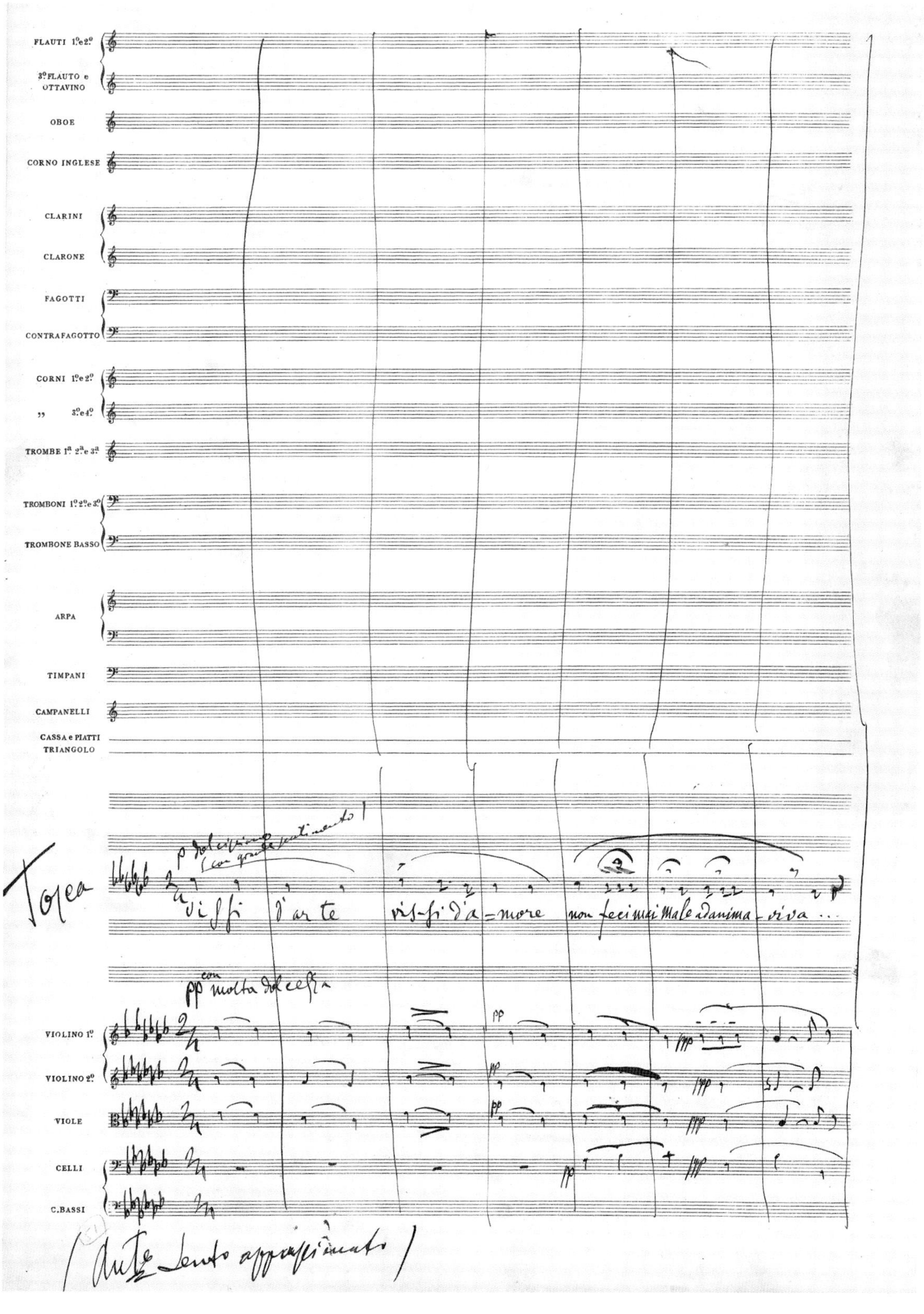

139—*Tosca* by Giacomo Puccini, aria *Vissi d'arte*, autograph score, 1900

140—*Il Ciro riconosciuto* by Niccolò Jommelli, autograph score, 1744
141—*Tamerlano* by Giovanni Simone Mayr, autograph score, 1812

Tamerlano

142—*A vucchella* by Francesco Paolo Tosti, lyrics by Gabriele D'Annunzio, autograph score, 1907

143—*I pini di Roma* by Ottorino Respighi, autograph score, 1924

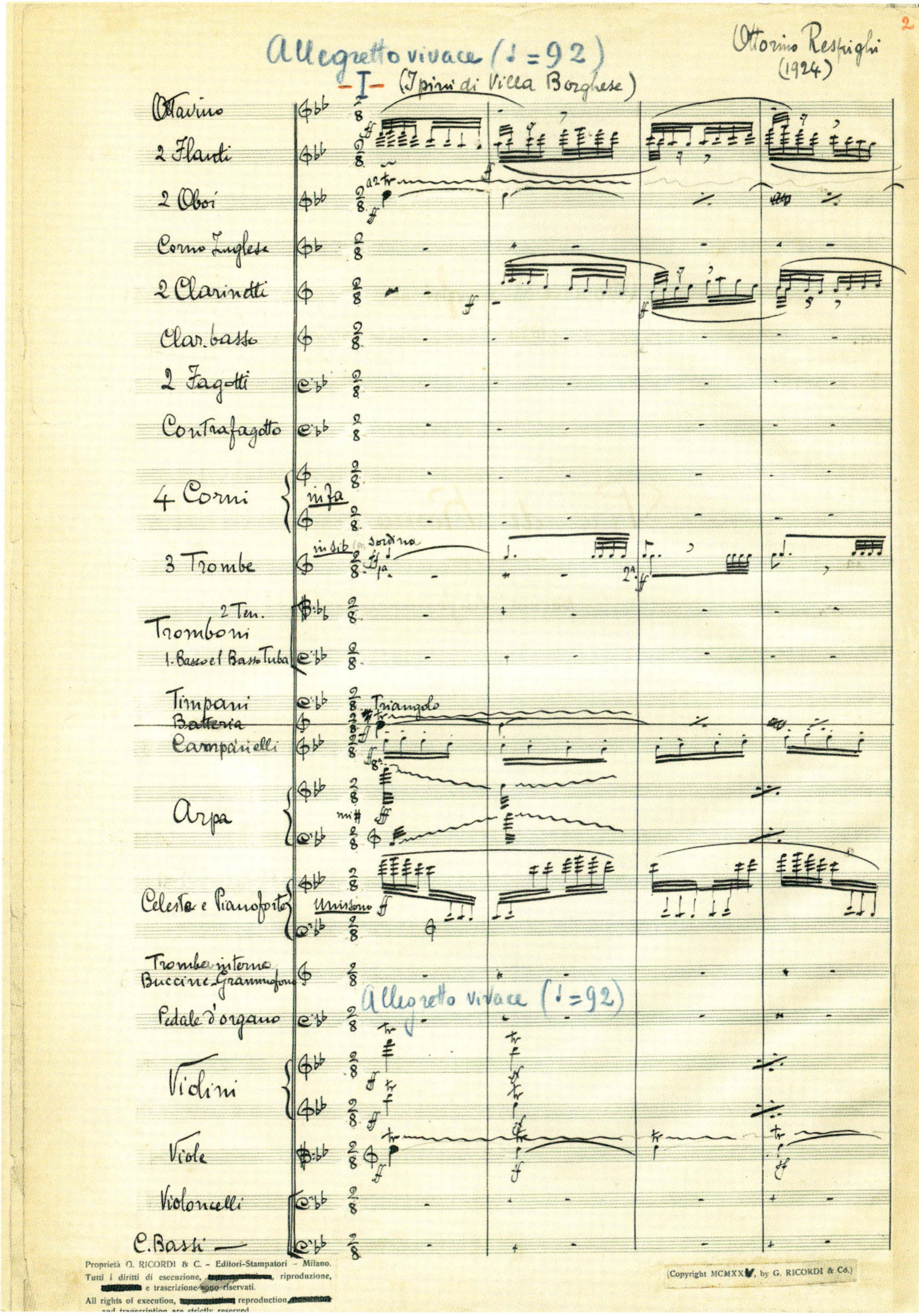
Allegretto vivace (♩=92)
-I- (I pini di Villa Borghese)
Ottorino Respighi
(1924)
Ottavino
2 Flauti
2 Oboi
Corno Inglese
2 Clarinetti
Clar. basso
2 Fagotti
Contrafagotto
4 Corni
3 Trombe
Tromboni
Timpani
Batteria
Triangolo
Campanelli
Arpa
Celesta e Pianoforte
Unisono
Tromba interna
Buccine Grammofono
Pedale d'organo
Allegretto vivace (♩=92)
Violini
Viole
Violoncelli
C. Bassi
Proprietà G. RICORDI & C. - Editori-Stampatori - Milano.
Tutti i diritti di esecuzione, riproduzione, e trascrizione sono riservati.
All rights of execution, reproduction and transcription are strictly reserved.
(Copyright MCMXXV, by G. RICORDI & Co.)

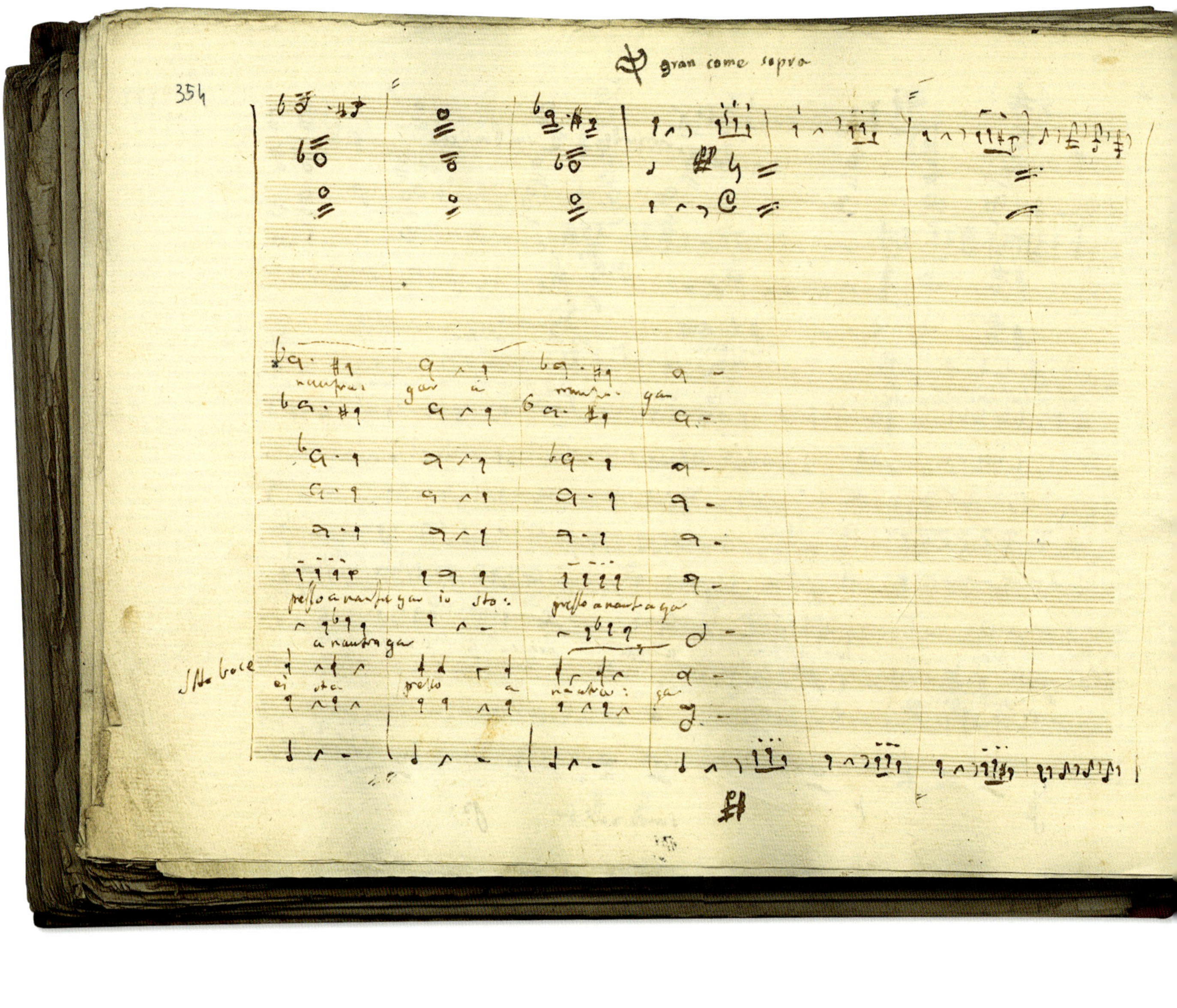

144—*L'italiana in Algeri* by Gioachino Rossini, aria *Nella testa ho un campanello*, autograph score, 1813

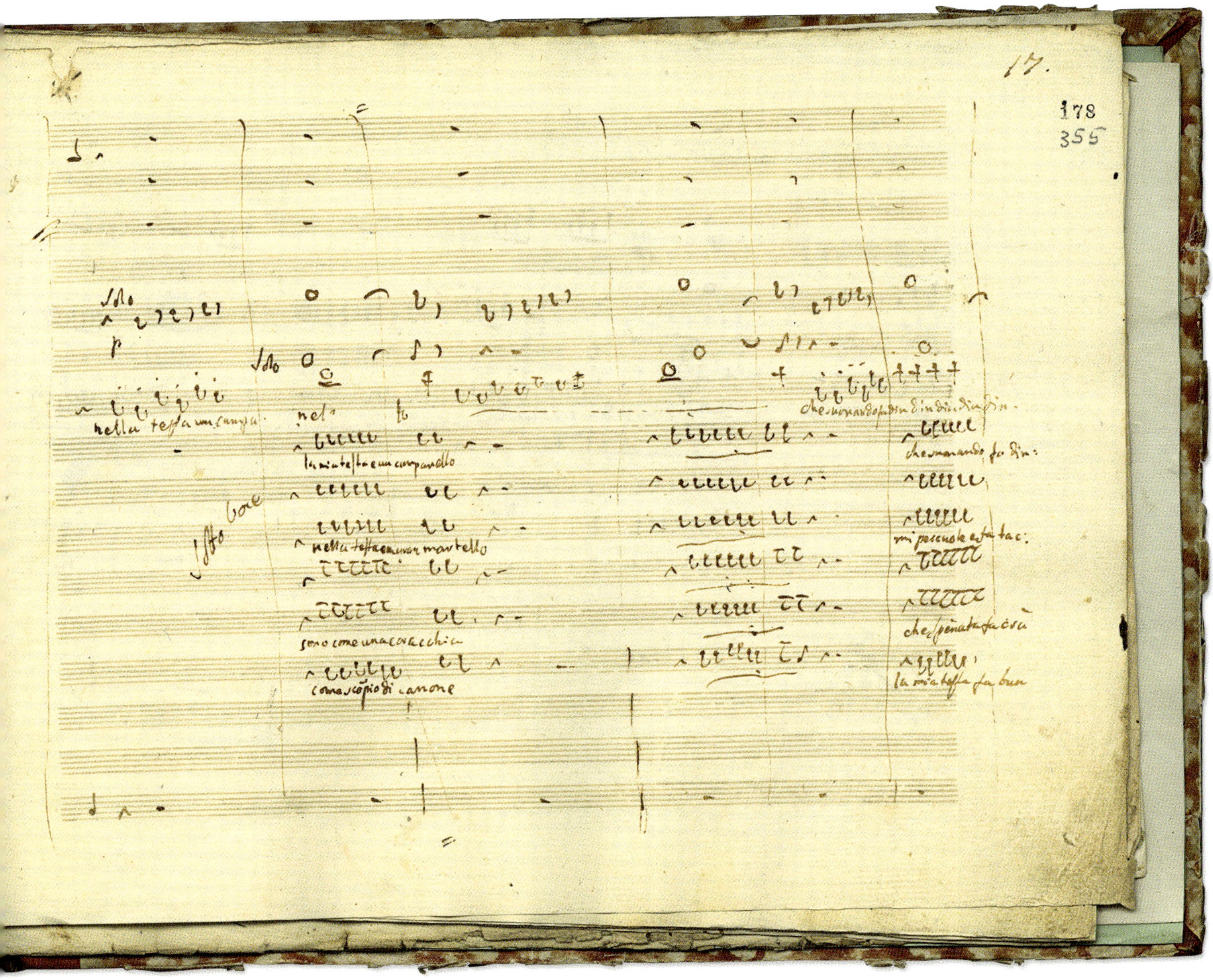

Printed Scores

In addition to the autographs, the archive also has an impressive collection of printed scores. Although not every edition has been preserved up to the present day, the existing material provides information about the development of music printing and matters of design, especially the jackets or covers, which were designed with love and care. Moreover, some editions contain dedications and comments from their users, such as conductors, that provide clues about their reception and interpretation.

145—*Miss America* by Vincenzo Billi, cover of the printed edition, 1925

146—*La voix humaine* by Francis Poulenc, cover of the printed edition, 1959

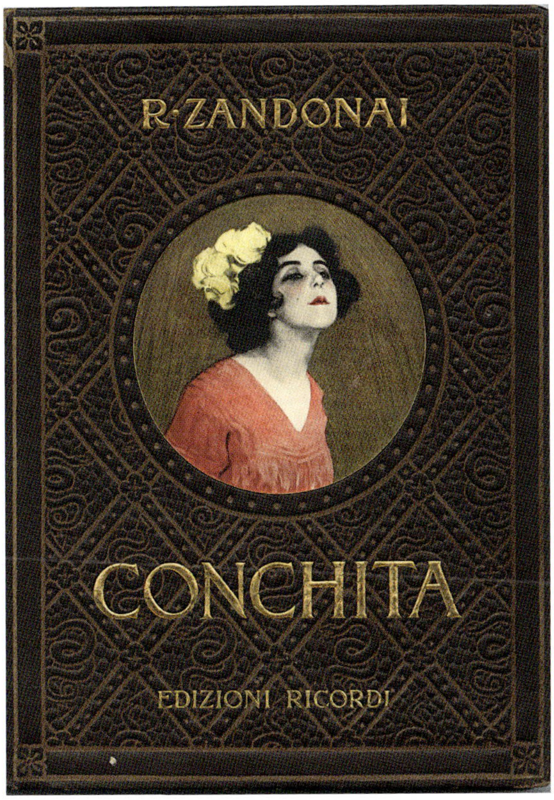

147—*Conchita* by Riccardo Zandonai, cover of the printed vocal score, 1911

148—*L'italiana in Algeri* by Gioachino Rossini, cover of the printed vocal score, 1898

149—*Bluff, fox trot di Ruggero Vitale*, artwork by Sergio Tofano, a.k.a. STO, 1922

150—*Tu! Melodia* by Pier Adolfo Tirindelli, artwork by Marcello Dudovich, 1907

Libretti

Over 10 000, from the 17th to 20th centuries. There are handwritten (even autograph) drafts, typed and printed libretto editions. Most of the libretti are printed editions, in the case of some operas there are several versions, from the premiere to editions of our time, from Italy and abroad.

The archive's libretto collection documents the purchase of the various other collections, such as that of La Scala, by Giovanni Ricordi; the influence of censorship; the development of the libretto in the 20th century, and much more.

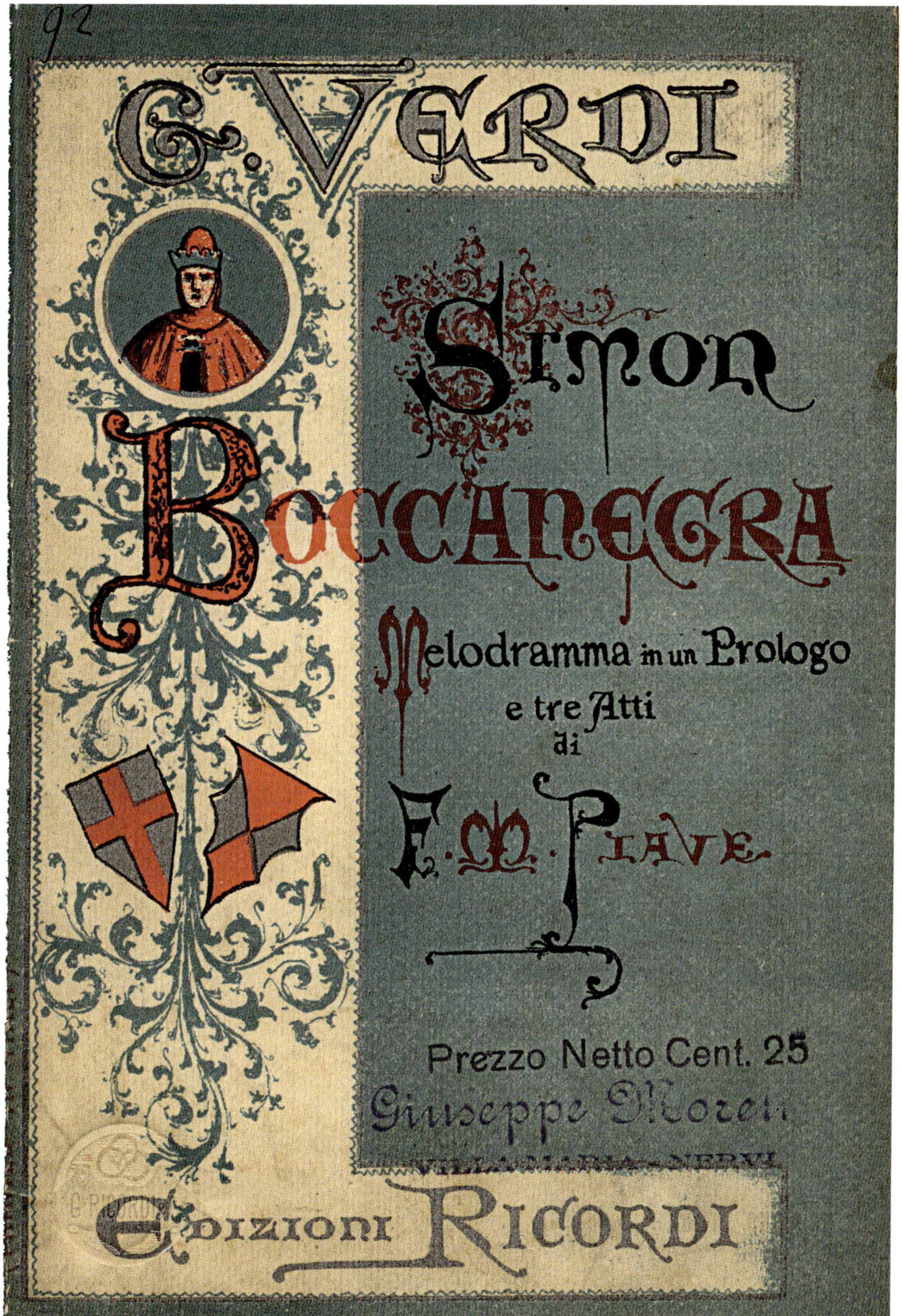

151—*Simon Boccanegra* by Giuseppe Verdi, cover of the libretto, second version, 1881

152—*Don Carlo* by Giuseppe Verdi, cover of the libretto, third edition

153—*La bohème* by Giacomo Puccini, page from the handwritten libretto with autograph annotations by Luigi Illica and Giacomo Puccini

154—*Iris* by Pietro Mascagni, cover of the libretto, artwork by Adolf Hohenstein, 1898

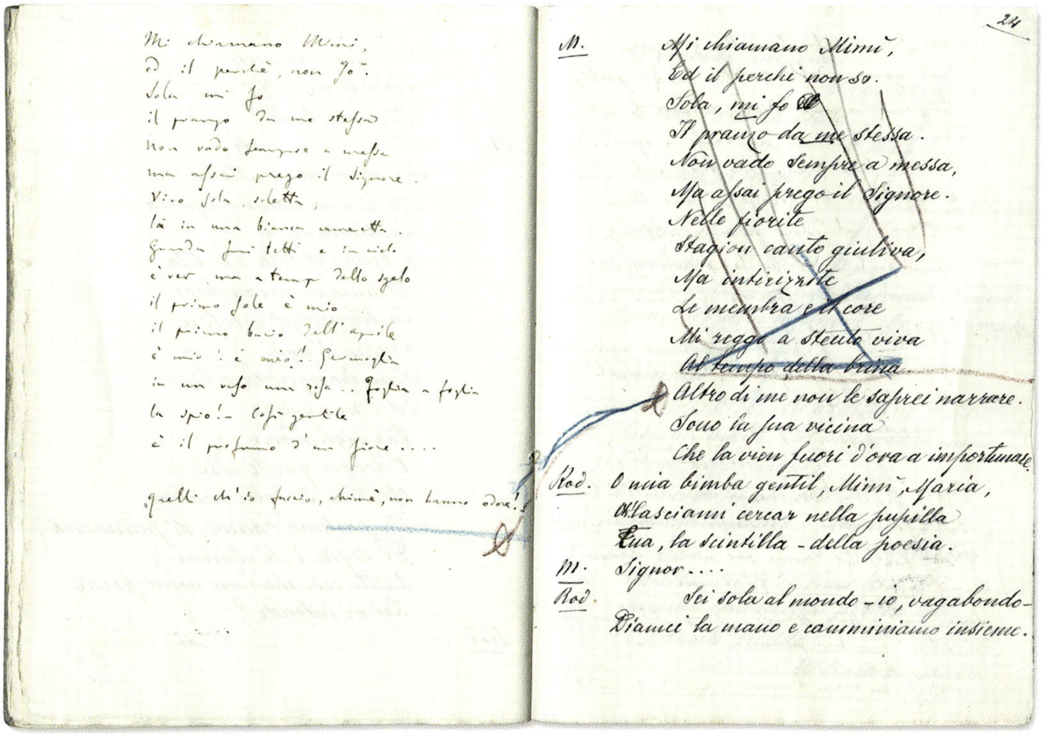

Mi chiamano Mimì,
ed il perchè, non so.
Sola mi fo
il pranzo da me stessa
Non vado sempre a messa
ma assai prego il Signore.
Vivo sola, soletta,
là in una bianca cameretta.
Guardo sui tetti e in cielo
è ver, ma a tempo dello sgelo
il primo sole è mio
il primo bacio dell'aprile
è mio! è mio!... Germoglia
in un vaso una rosa... foglia a foglia
la spio!... così gentile
è il profumo d'un fiore...

quelli ch'io faccio, ahimè, non hanno odore!

24

M. Mi chiamano Mimì,
Ed il perchè non so.
Sola, mi fo
Il pranzo da me stessa.
Non vado sempre a messa,
Ma assai prego il Signore.
Nelle fiorite
Stagioni canto giuliva,
Ma intirizzite
Le membra e il core
Mi reggo a stento viva
Al tempo della brina.
Altro di me non le saprei narrare.
Sono la sua vicina
Che la vien fuori d'ora a importunare.
Rod. O mia bimba gentil, Mimì, Maria,
Ah lasciami cercar nella pupilla
Tua, la scintilla - della poesia.
M. Signor....
Rod. Sei sola al mondo - io, vagabondo -
Dammi la mano e camminiamo insieme.

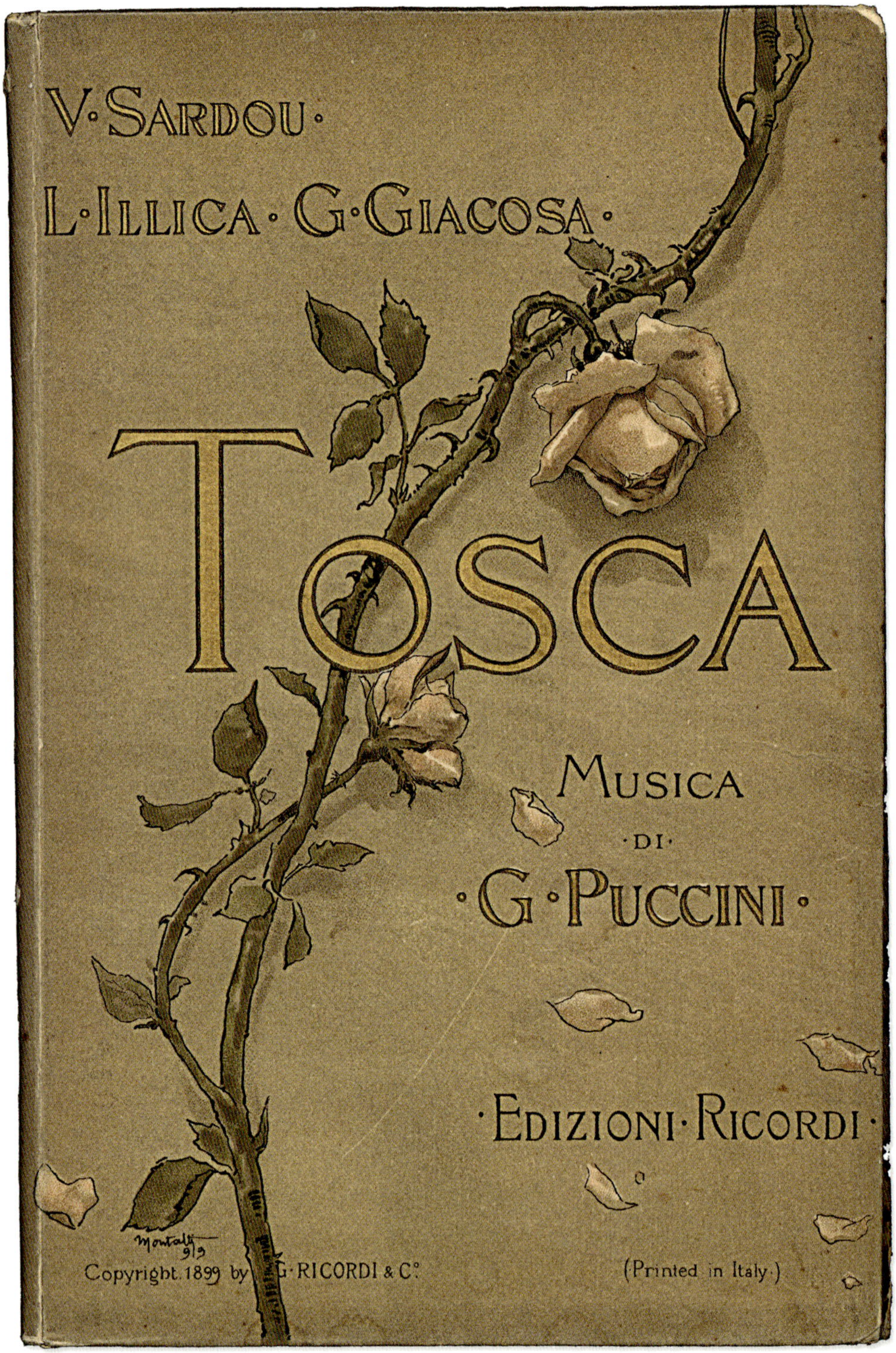

155—*Tosca* by Giacomo Puccini, cover of the libretto for the world premiere, 1900

156—*Germania* by Alberto Franchetti, cover of the libretto, artwork by Adolf Hohenstein, 1902

L. ILLICA
GERMANIA
DRAMMA LIRICO
MUSICA DI A. FRANCHETTI
EDIZIONI RICORDI
IIa EDIZIONE
(Printed in Italy)
(Imprimé en Italie)

Visual Arts Collection

The archive's visual arts collection is from the 19th and 20th centuries. The archive has about 600 original stage designs, mostly from the premieres of the respective works, starting with the designs for Verdi's *Attila* by Giuseppe Bertoja up to Nicola Benois's designs for Respighi's *La Fiamma* from the 1930s. The technique is usually tempera painting, but there are also designs in oils, or made as collages. For some operas there are different variations, such as for Puccini's *Tosca* and *La bohème*, depending on the size of the intended theater.

Furthermore, the picture collection consists of a collection of thousands of individual costume designs, most of them created by famous designers. It begins with the figurines for Verdi's *Il Corsaro* (1848) and comprises more than 1200 designs by Alfredo Edel, including for Verdi's operas *Il Trovatore, Don Carlos* and *Otello* and Rossini's *Guglielmo Tell*. There are more than 700 items by Adolf Hohenstein. The costume designs are often accompanied by instructions for the dressmakers on the back, and by fabric and color patterns, for the Italian operas, but also for foreign-language works from abroad (for example in Cyrillic script for *Una vita per lo Zar* by Mikhail Glinka, and for Franz Gaul's designs for the operas of Wagner).

Finally, the "tavole di attrezzeria", drawn summaries of props and stage furniture, of which about 500 are preserved in the archive, should be mentioned.

157—*Don Carlo* by Giuseppe Verdi, Modena, December 26, 1886. *The forest of Fontainebleau*, Act I, set design by Carlo Ferrario

N°21.
Rienzi
Invitato Ungherese Gesandter der Ungarn
(Corifeo)

37
Bailadora de Pandero

Filippo II
15

Donne e Ragazze Atto Primo

158—*Rienzi* by Richard Wagner. *Hungarian guest*, costume design by Franz Gaul, 1872

159—*Anima allegra* by Franco Vittadini, world premiere, Rome, Teatro Costanzi, 1921. *Bailadora de pandero*, costume design by Marco Montedoro

160—*Don Carlo* by Giuseppe Verdi, new version in 4 acts, Milan, Teatro alla Scala, 1884. *Filippo II*, Act I, costume design by Alfredo Edel

161—*Una vita per lo Zar* by Mikhail Ivanovic Glinka, Italian premiere, Milan, Teatro Dal Verme, 1874. *Women and girls*, Act I, costume design by anonymous

162—*Il corsaro* by Giuseppe Verdi, world premiere, Trieste, Teatro Grande, 1848. *Odalisque*, costume design by Damore

163—*Il ragno azzurro* by Alberto Igino Randegger, Milan, 1918. *Dancers*, costume design by Aroldo Bonzagni

164—*Aida* by Giuseppe Verdi, new production, Milan, Teatro alla Scala, 1904. *Incense bearer*, costume design by Attilio Comelli

165—*Il trillo del diavolo* by Stanislao Falchi, world premiere, Rome, Teatro Argentina, 1899. *Venetian patricians*, Act I, costume design by Alfredo Edel.

Il favorito del re by Antonio Veretti, world premiere, Milan, Teatro alla Scala, 1932

166—*Lalla*, Act I, costume design by Titina Rota

167—*A lady*, Act I, costume design by Titina Rota

Nerone by Arrigo Boito, posthumous world premiere, Milan, Teatro alla Scala, 1924.

168—*Gobrias*, costume design by Lodovico Pogliaghi

169—*Necklace and earrings*, prop design by Lodovico Pogliaghi

170—*Francesca da Rimini* by Riccardo Zandonai, world premiere, Turin, Teatro Regio, 1914. *Paolo and Francesca*, Act II, costume design by Luigi Sapelli a.k.a. Caramba

171—*La leggenda di Sakùntala* by Franco Alfano, world premiere, Bologna, Teatro Comunale, 1921 *Sakùntala*, Act II and III, costume design by Daniele Crespi

172—*Mefistofele* by Arrigo Boito, Milan, Teatro alla Scala, 1881. *Prologue in Heaven*, set design by Carlo Ferrario

173—*Germania* by Alberto Franchetti, world premiere, Milan, Teatro alla Scala, 1902. *Epilogue, Federico in Ricke's arms,* in the background Napoleon's army in retreat, drawing by Leopoldo Metlicovitz

GERMANIA DI A·FRANCHETTI

EPILOGO

Photographs

Photographs form another collection of images in the archive. There are over 6000 photographs from the late 19th and 20th centuries: studio portraits, and shots of scenes and exteriors. The material in general is linked to the activity of Casa Ricordi and comprises portraits of composers, librettists, actors, dancers, singers (in costume or not, thus giving an insight into the fashion of the time). The photos often have a dedication on the mount.

The photographers (over 800 names) are Italian, like Ferrario, Bertieri, Varischi & Artico, Sommariva, De Marchi, Pagliano e Ricordi, Rossi, Sciutto, Sebastianutti, as well as foreign: photos from Studio Nadar, Reutlinger, London studios (Wilson & C., Ellis), American studios, studios at Leipzig, St Petersburg, Vienna, Cairo, Marseille, Budapest, São Paulo and so on. Some composers and designers were also dilettante photographers, as Giacomo Puccini (for example his snapshots in Egypt or Abetone, near Pistoia) and Leopoldo Metlicovitz. Many photographs were used to illustrate the Ricordi magazines, such as *Musica e Musicisti* and *Ars et Labor.*

Finally, the archive also has a large collection of about 200 prints, primarily portraits of musicians and singers that were originally filed with the photographs, but now form a separate department.

174—Eleonora Duse, photograph by Mario Nunes Vais, early 20th century

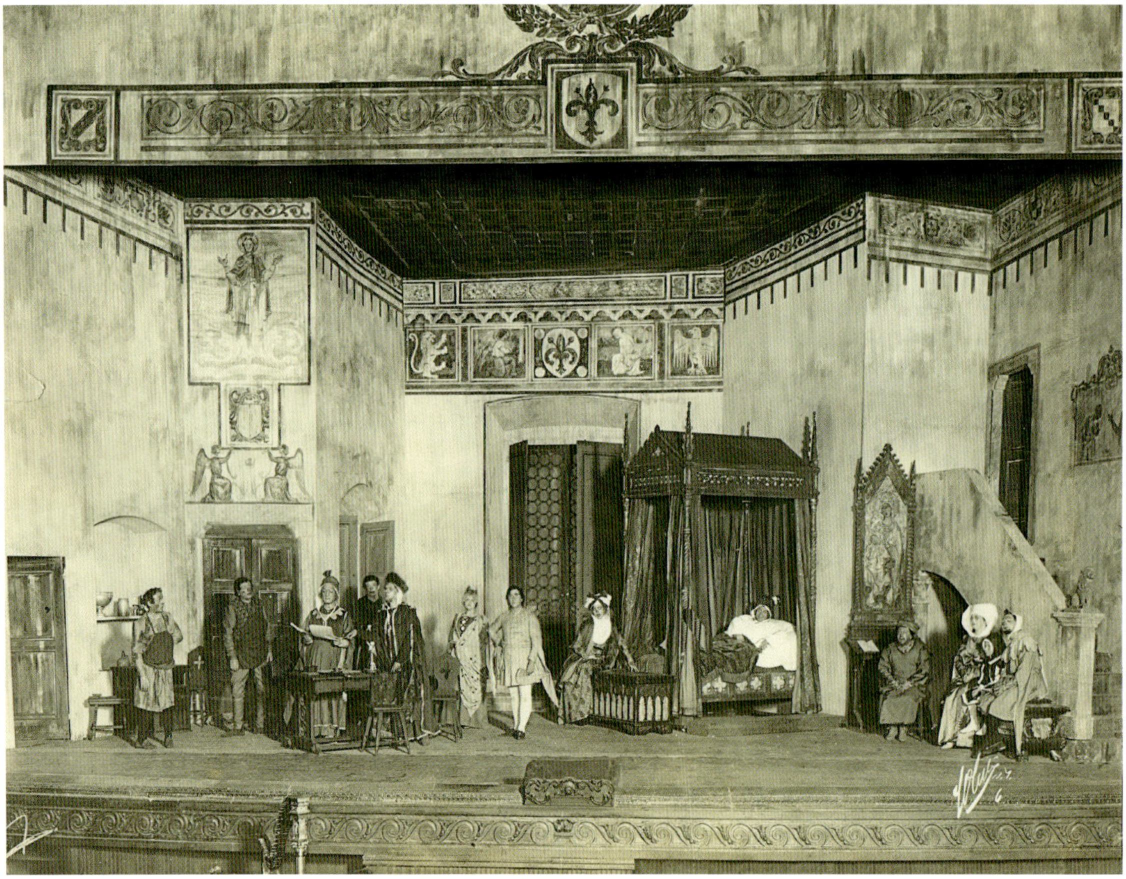

175—The cast of the world premiere of *Gianni Schicchi* by Giacomo Puccini, on stage, 1918
176—A scene from *La bohème* by Giacomo Puccini, *Barrière d'Enfer*, Act III, 1896

177 —Garden of the villa in Sant'Agata, (from left, seated) Maria Carrara Verdi, Barberina Strepponi, Giuseppe Verdi, Giuditta Ricordi, (from left, standing) Teresa Stolz, Umberto Campanari, Giulio Ricordi, Leopoldo Metlicovitz, late 19th century

178 —Actress Sarah Bernhardt in stage costume, photograph by Nadar, late 19th century

179—Giacomo Puccini
on the Brooklyn Bridge
in New York, 1910

Posters

The image collection also includes a collection of posters from the turn of the century and the beginning of the 20th century. These constitute an important documentation of the activity of Casa Ricordi in the field of graphics. At that time, Casa Ricordi was one of the few publishers in the world that was able to print large posters and it even received orders from overseas.

The collection consists not only of posters for opera performances, but also for *Bitter Campari, Poretti* beer, *Uliveto* water, the *Bianchi* bicycle brand, the *La Rinascente* department store and the *Corriere della Sera*. Particularly noteworthy are the series of posters for the film *Cabiria* from 1914 (directed by Giovanni Pastrone) and those for the *Magazzini Mele* in Naples. The Officine Grafiche also designed the covers of the Ricordi publishing house's music editions, which are therefore of considerable beauty and originality.

180—Giacomo Puccini, *Turandot,* Milan, Teatro alla Scala, 1926. Poster for the world premiere, artwork by Leopoldo Metlicovitz

181—*Manifesto* by Leopoldo Metlicovitz for *La Rinascente*, 1913

182—Poster by Marcello Dudovich for *Acqua Uliveto*, 1906

CAMPARI
Bitter
DAVIDE
CAMPARI
&C.
MILANO
BITTER
CAMPARI

183—Poster by Vespasiano Bignami, for the world premiere of *Manon Lescaut* by Giacomo Puccini, 1893

LESCAUT
PUCCINI

Letters

The collection of manuscript letters — about 15 000 of them — covers the time from the beginning of the 19th century until the end of the 20th century. It consists of letters to Casa Ricordi by writers, singers and composers including Giuseppe Verdi, Giacomo Puccini, Franz Liszt, Ottorino Respighi, Jules Massenet, Alfredo Casella and Luigi Nono; the librettists Luigi Illica, Giuseppe Giacosa and Arrigo Boito; the poet Gabriele d'Annunzio; and the singers Teresa Stolz, Maria Waldmann and Victor Maurel. There are also extensive further collections from the 20th century, both manuscript and typewritten: letters by Gian Francesco Malipiero (1942—1954), Ildebrando Pizzetti (1942—1956), Vieri Tosatti (1949—1960) and Mario Zafred (1950—1956), letters from Tito I and Giulio, and numerous letters associated with specific works.

The "copialettere", the business correspondence, form the second part of the collection of letters. They are complete from 1888 to 1962, with some gaps from 1944 to 1953. Each financial year is divided into several volumes. An index volume lists the addressees. The "copialettere" enable the reconstruction of correspondence, as was the case for the letters to Arturo Toscanini, for example.

184—Envelope of a letter from Giuseppe Verdi to Giulio Ricordi, December 26, 1893

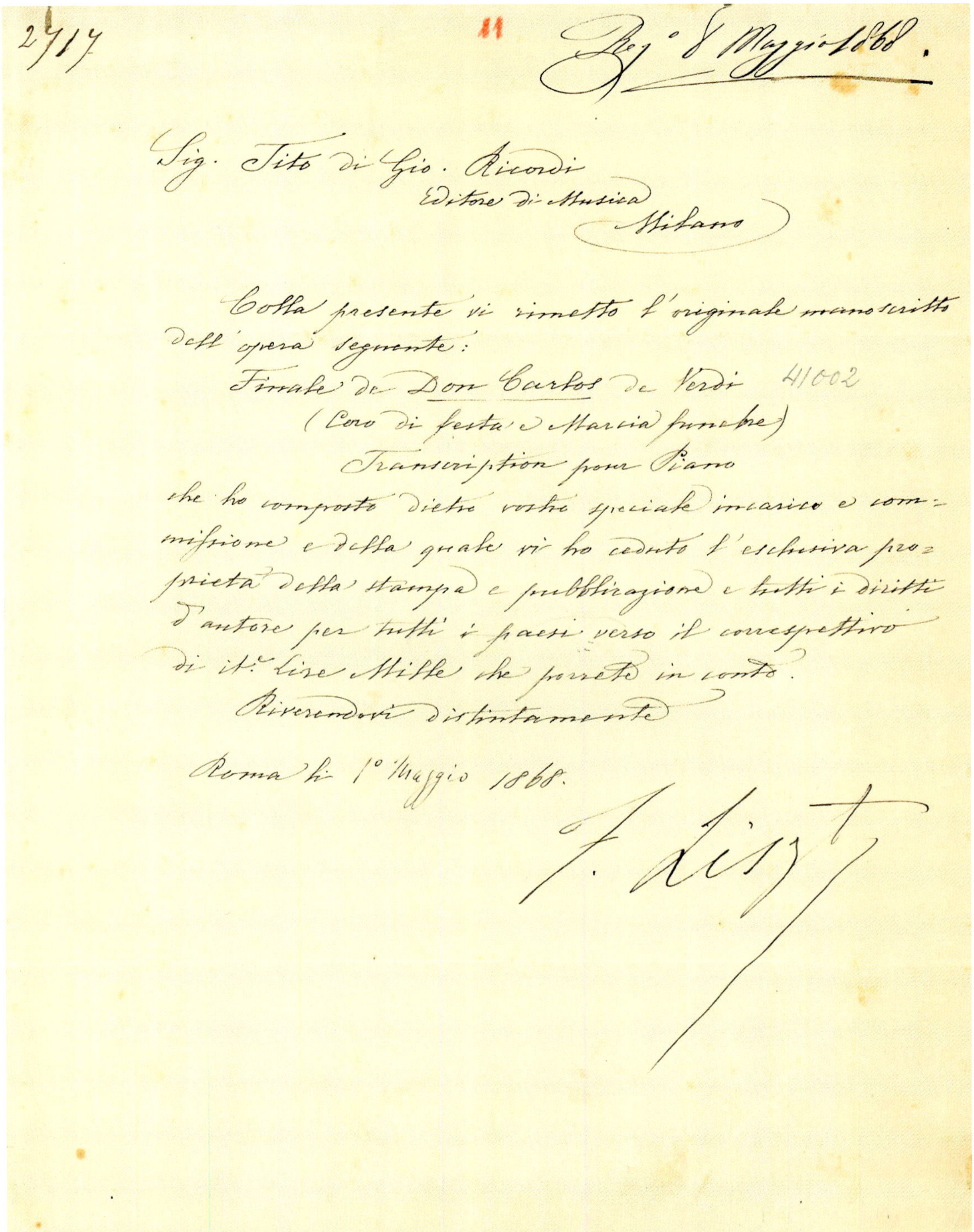

2717 11 Reg.° 8 Maggio 1868.

Sig. Tito di Gio. Ricordi
Editore di Musica
Milano

Colla presente vi rimetto l'originale manoscritto dell'opera seguente:

Finale de Don Carlos de Verdi 41002
(Coro di festa e Marcia funebre)
Transcription pour Piano

che ho composto dietro vostro speciale incarico e commissione e della quale vi ho ceduto l'esclusiva proprietà della stampa e pubblicazione e tutti i diritti d'autore per tutti i paesi verso il corrispettivo di it.e lire Mille che porrete in conto.

Riverendovi distintamente

Roma li 1° Maggio 1868.

F. Liszt

185—A letter/contract (1868) from Franz Liszt which grants Tito I Ricordi the exclusive rights to his composition *Finale de Don Carlos de Verdi*, which would be published with plate number 41002; the autograph score is conserved in the Archive

186—Giacomo Puccini, pleased about the great success of his opera Manon Lescaut in America, writes to Tito II Ricordi "New York is extraordinary!", 1907

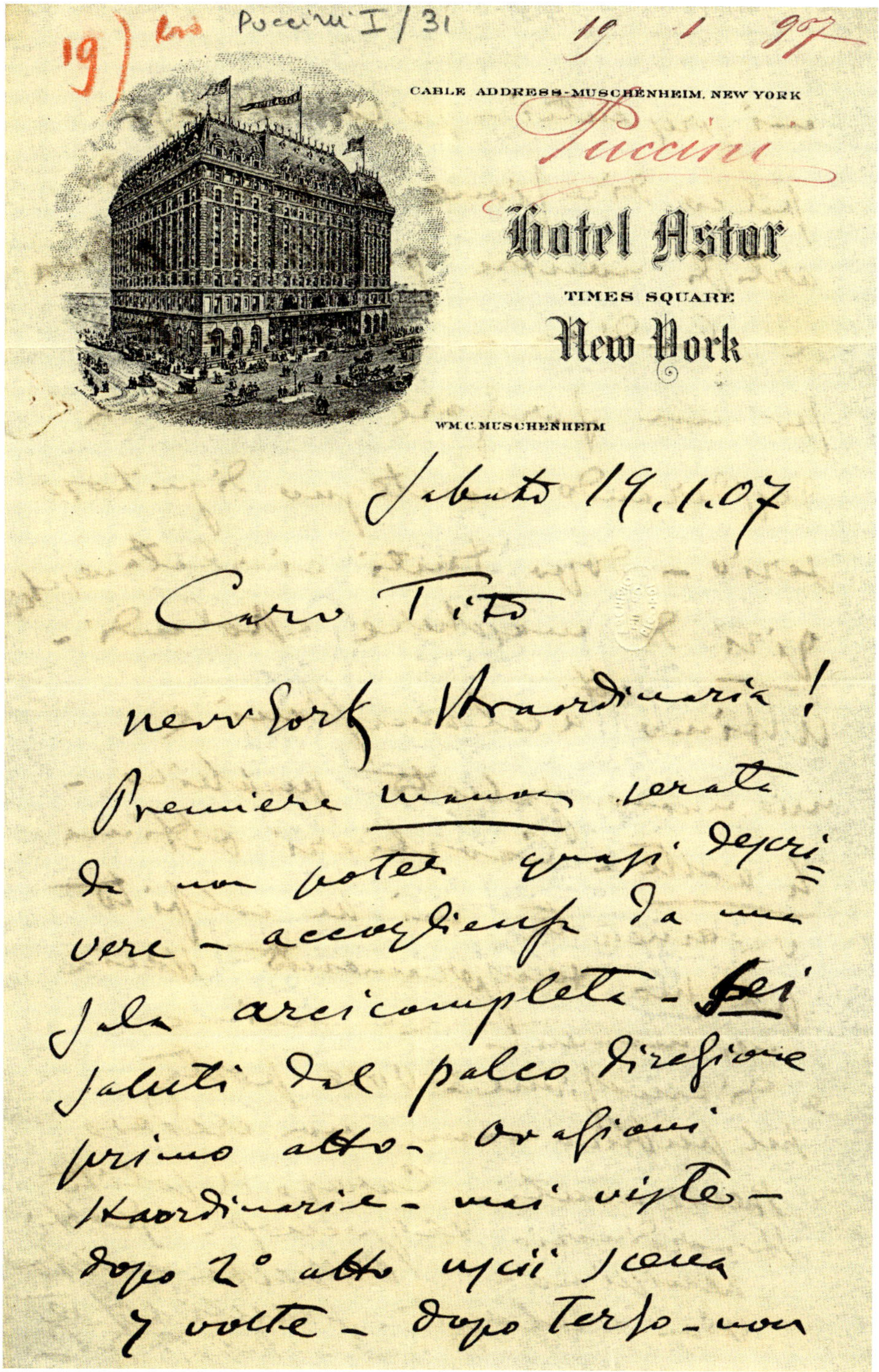

19) Puccini I/31 19 1 907

CABLE ADDRESS-MUSCHENHEIM, NEW YORK

Puccini

Hotel Astor

TIMES SQUARE

New York

WM.C.MUSCHENHEIM

Sabato 19.1.07

Caro Tito

New York straordinaria!

Première ~~[illegible]~~ serata da non potersi descrivere – accoglienze da una sala arcicompleta – Sei saluti dal palco direzione primo atto – ovazioni straordinarie – mai viste – dopo 2° atto uscii scena 7 volte – dopo Terzo – non

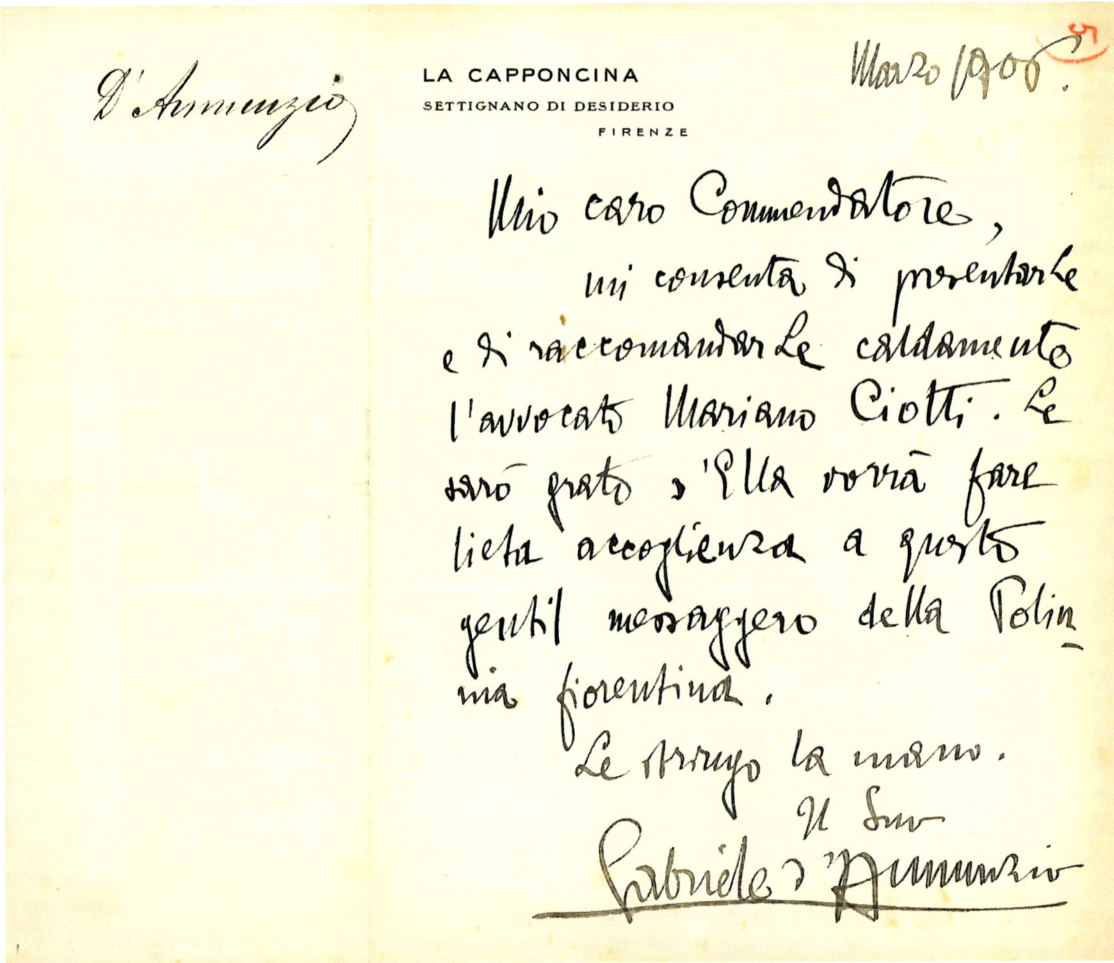

D'Annunzio

LA CAPPONCINA
SETTIGNANO DI DESIDERIO
FIRENZE

Marzo 1906.

Mio caro Commendatore,

mi consenta di presentarle e di raccomandarLe caldamente l'avvocato Mariano Ciotti. Le sarò grato s'Ella vorrà fare lieta accoglienza a questo gentil messaggero della Polinnia fiorentina.

Le stringo la mano.

Il suo

Gabriele d'Annunzio

187—A letter from the poet and dramaturge Gabriele D'Annunzio asking Ricordi to receive the lawyer Mariano Ciotti in Milan, 1906

188—A humorous letter from the librettistandcomposerArrigo BoitotoJulesBurgmein,nomde plume of the publisher Giulio Ricordi, to whom Boito promises a meal should he not complete his opera *Nerone* by the 29th, indeed the 28th, of February 1881. In fact he never did finish the opera, which would be performed posthumously in 1924

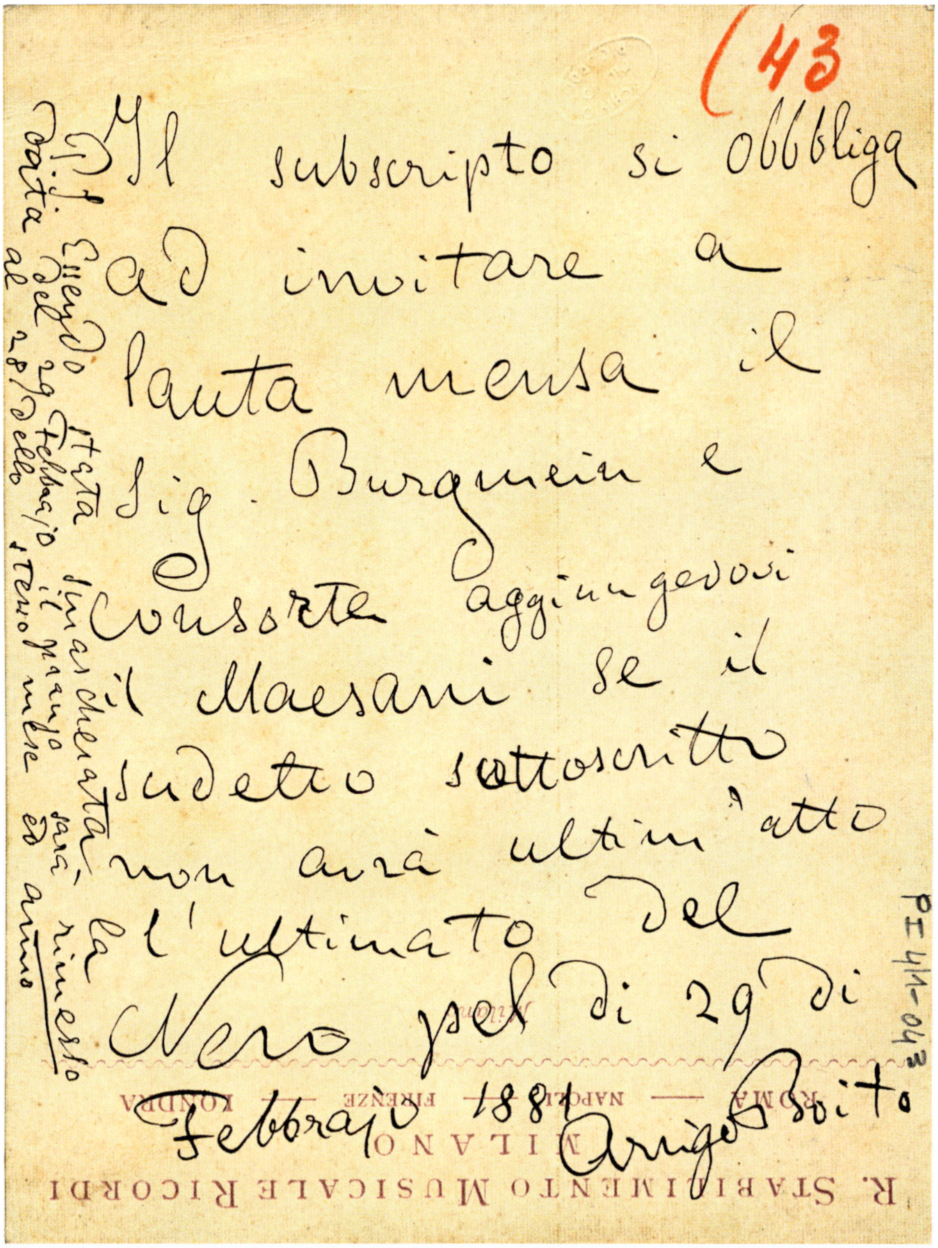

(43

Il subscripto si obbbliga
ad invitare a
lauta mensa il
Sig. Burgmein e
Consorte aggiungedovi
il Maesani se il
sudetto sottoscritto
non avrà ultim'atto
l'ultimato del
Nero pel di 29 di
Febbrajo 1881
Arrigo Boito

P.S. Essendo stata una mascherata la rimesso
data del 29 Febbrajo il giorno sarà
al 28 dello stesso mese ed anno

R. Stabilimento Musicale Ricordi
Milano
Roma — Napoli — Firenze — Londra

Administrative Documents

The archive includes documents about the history of the publishing house from the 200 years of its existence. First of all, we have Giovanni Ricordi's "libri mastri", which span the time from 1814 until the mid-19th century and which summarize and document all contracts concluded.

There are also documents from the 100-year existence of the company's copperplate engraving school; handwritten lists of all editions acquired by Ricordi from 1808 until the present day; a large number of the publishing catalogs published by Ricordi and by the publishers bought up by Ricordi; press reviews with a collection of reviews; original contracts with composers and librettists including Giuseppe Verdi, Giacomo Puccini,Franco Alfano, Gian Carlo Menotti, Arrigo Boito, Luigi Illica, Sem Benelli and Arturo Rossato.

Finally, there are documents that show Giovanni and Tito Ricordi's commitment to copyright for authors: newspaper clippings, articles and letters. One cultural-historical curiosity to be admired in the archive is the collection of lead printing plates from the 19th century.

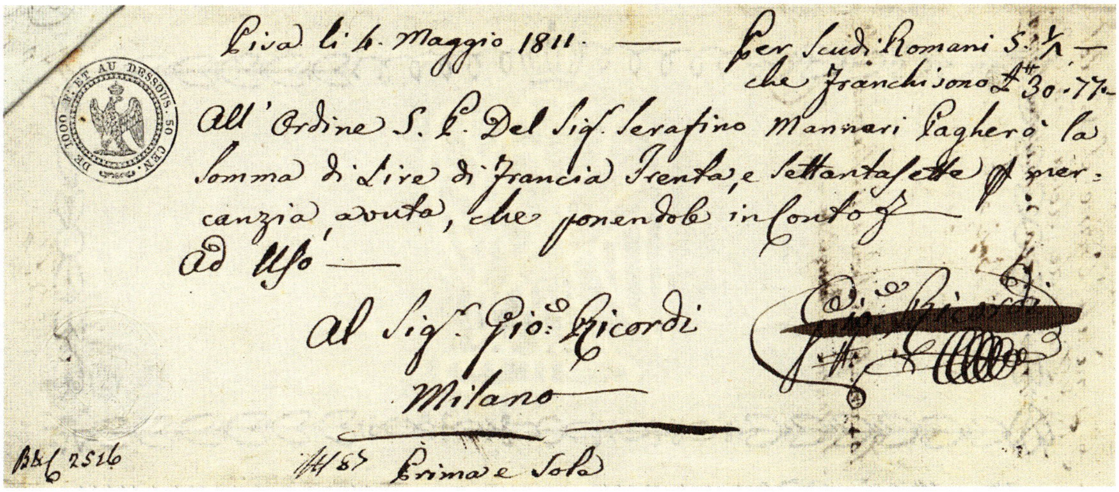

Pisa li 4. Maggio 1811 — Per Scudi Romani 5.½ —
che Franchi sono L.te 30.77 —
All'Ordine S. P. Del Sig. Serafino Mannari Pagherò la
somma di Lire di Francia Trenta, e settantasette % per
canzia avuta, che ponendole in Conto &
ad Uso —
Al Sig.r Gio: Ricordi
Milano
Prima e Sola

189—Promissory note to Giovanni Ricordi, for the purchase of musical material, Pisa, May 4, 1811

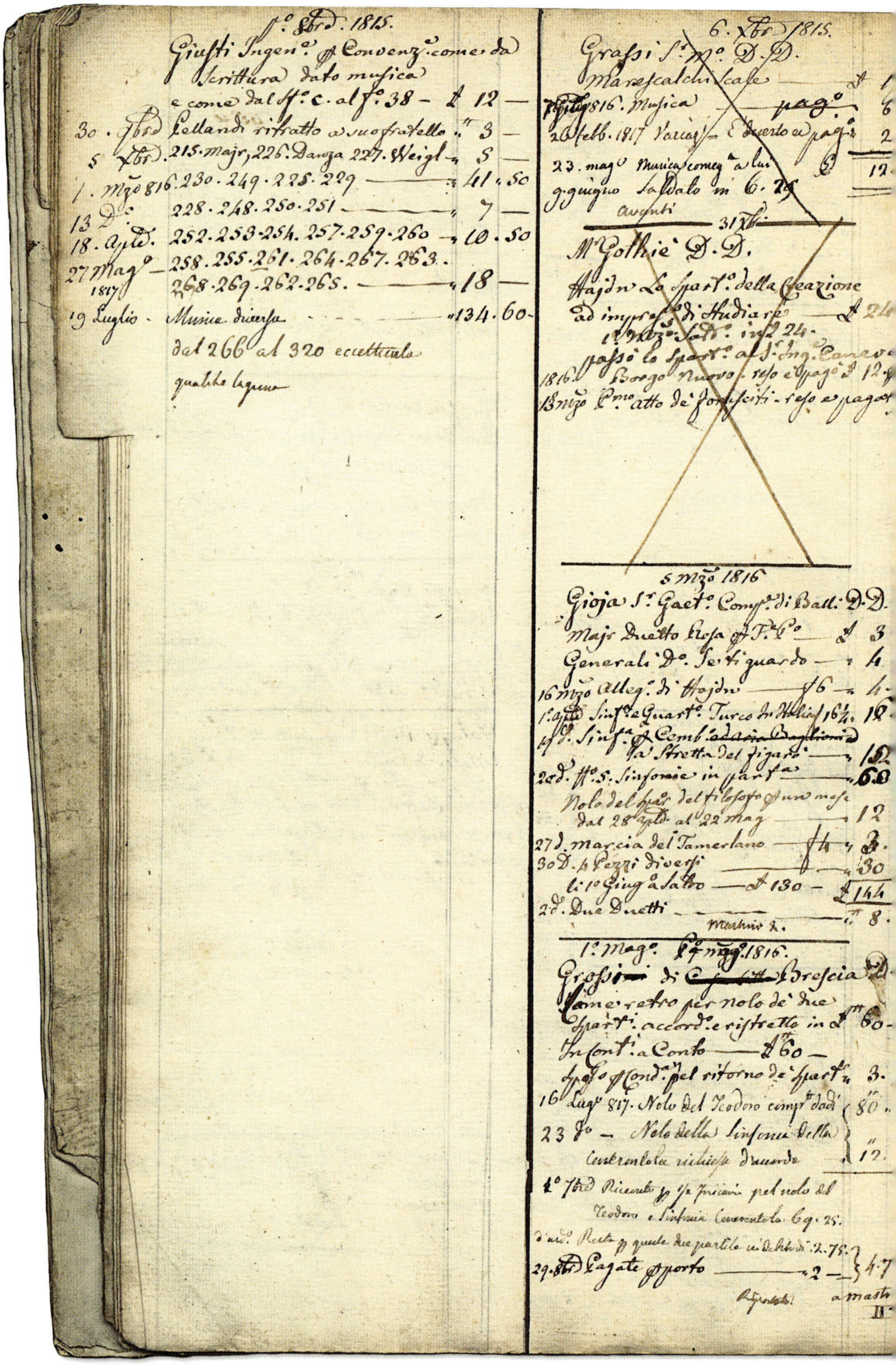

190—Page of the so-called "mastrino" ledger, kept by Giovanni Ricordi, concerning years 1814—1816

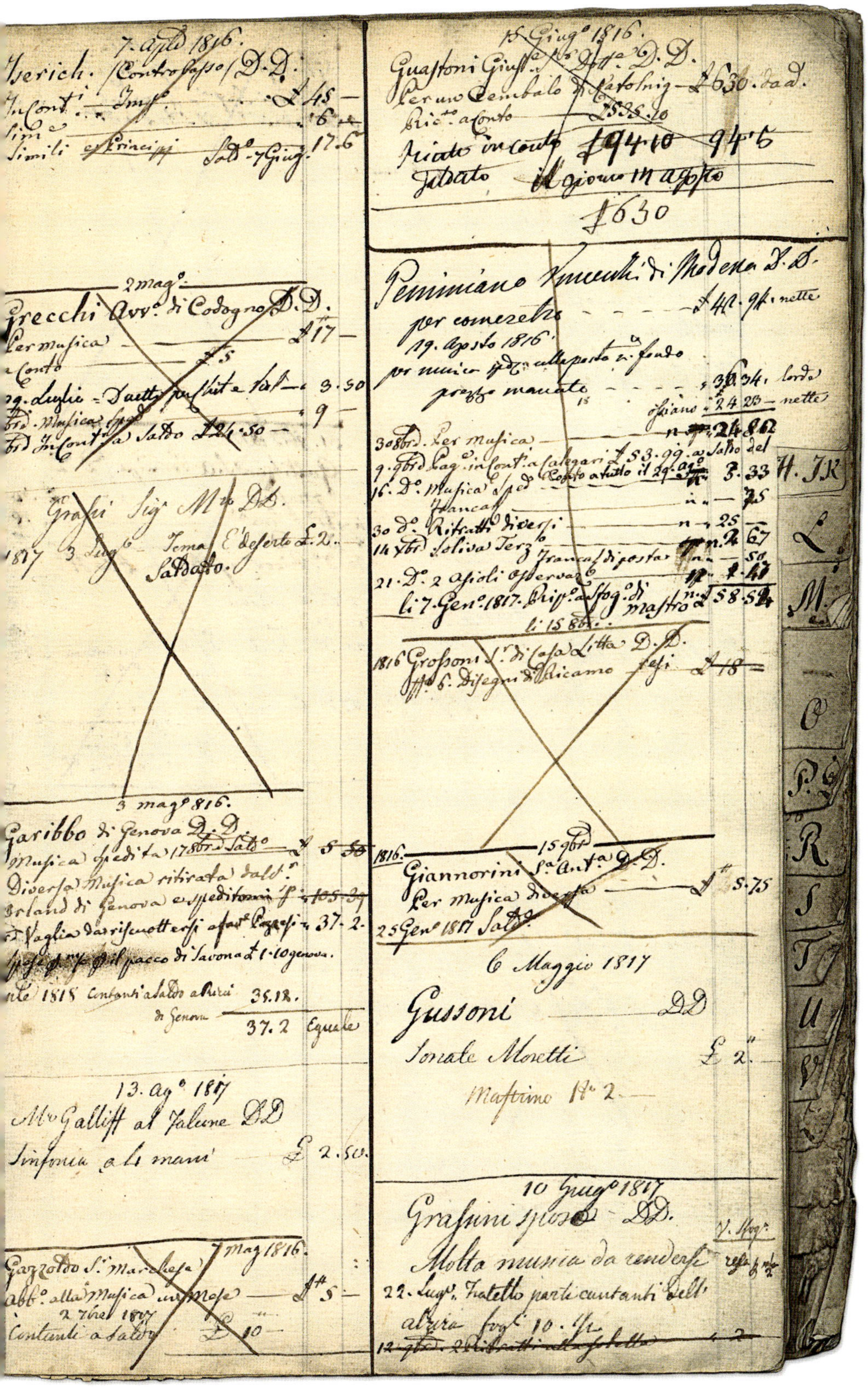

7. Aprile 1816.
...erich. Contrabasso / D.D.
In Cont.° ... £ 45
Simili ... 6
Simili e Principij Sald.° 7 Giug.° 17.6

2 mag.°
...ecchi Avv.° di Codogno D.D.
Per musica £ 17
a Conto 5
29. Luglio ... 3.50
... Musica sped.ª 9
... In Cont.° a Saldo £ 24.50

... Grassi Sig.r M.° D.D.
1817 3 Lug.° Tema E deserto £ 2.
Saldato.

3 mag.° 1816.
Garibbo di Genova D.D.
Musica spedita 17 8bre Sald.° £ 5 50
Diversa Musica ritirata dal ...
... di Genova e speditomi ... 105 ...
... Vaglia da riscuotersi ... 37. 2.
... del pacco di Savona £ 1.10 genova.
...1818 Contanti a saldo ... di Genova 35.18.
37. 2 Eguale

13. Ag.° 1817
M.° Galliff al Falcone D.D.
Sinfonia a 4 mani £ 2.50.

7 Mag 1816.
Gazzoldo S.r Marchese
abb.° alla Musica un Mese £ 5
2 7bre 1817
Contanti a Saldo £ 10

15 Giug.° 1816.
Guastoni Giusep.e ... D.D.
Per un Cembalo di ... £ 630. da d.
Ric.to a Conto 535.10
Ricato in Conto £ 94.10 94.6
Saldato il giorno 11 agosto
£ 630

Perniciano Vincenzo di Modena D.D.
per concerti ... £ 41. 9 f. nette
19. Agosto 1816.
per musica sped.a alla posta di fondo
prezzo mancato ... 30.34. lordo
... 24 23 — nette
30 8bre. Per musica ... 24.82
9 9bre Pag.° in Cont.° a Calegari £ 53.99. a Saldo del
Conto a tutto il 29. ... 3. 33
16. D.° Musica sped.ª francat.ª ... 75
30 d.° Ritratti diversi ... 25
14 Xbre Solisa Terz. ... francatura di posta ... 2. 67
... 50
21. D.° 2 ... Osservaz.e ... 1. 41
li 7. Gen.° 1817. Ricev.ª al fog.° di mastro ... 58.52
li 15 ...

1816 Grossoni S.r di Casa Litta D.D.
... 6. Disegni di Ricamo ... £ 18

1816. 15 9bre
Giannorini S.a Ant.a D.D.
Per Musica diversa £ 5.75
25 Gen.° 1817 Sald.°

6 Maggio 1817
Gussoni D.D.
Sonate Moretti £ 2.
Mastrino N.° 2.

10 Giug.° 1817
Grassini sposo D.D.
Molta musica da rendersi
22. Lug.° Fratello parti cantanti dell'
altra fog.° 10. ...
12 ... 2

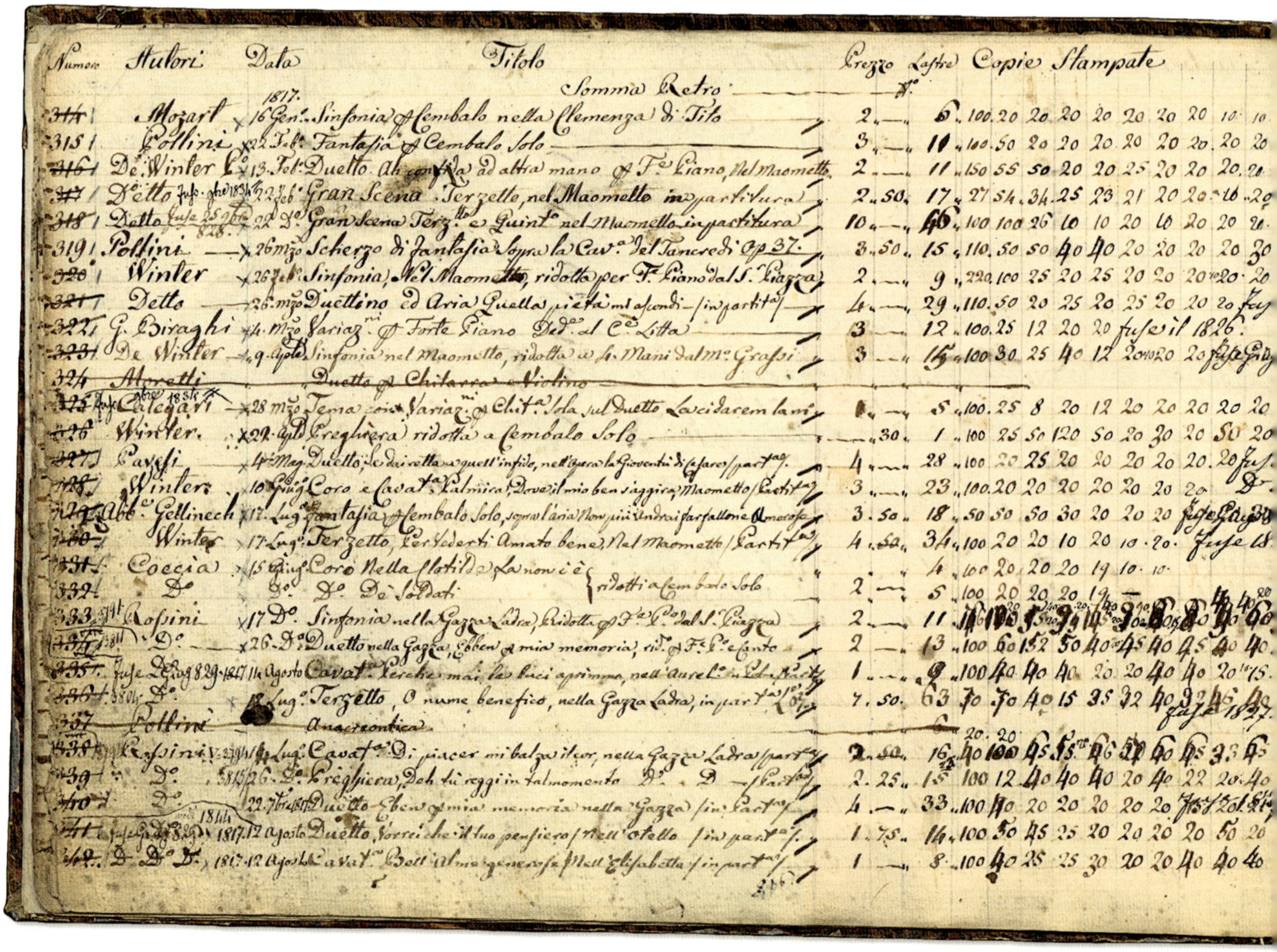

191—Page of one of the so-called "libroni", production ledgers of the new compositions acquired by Casa Ricordi

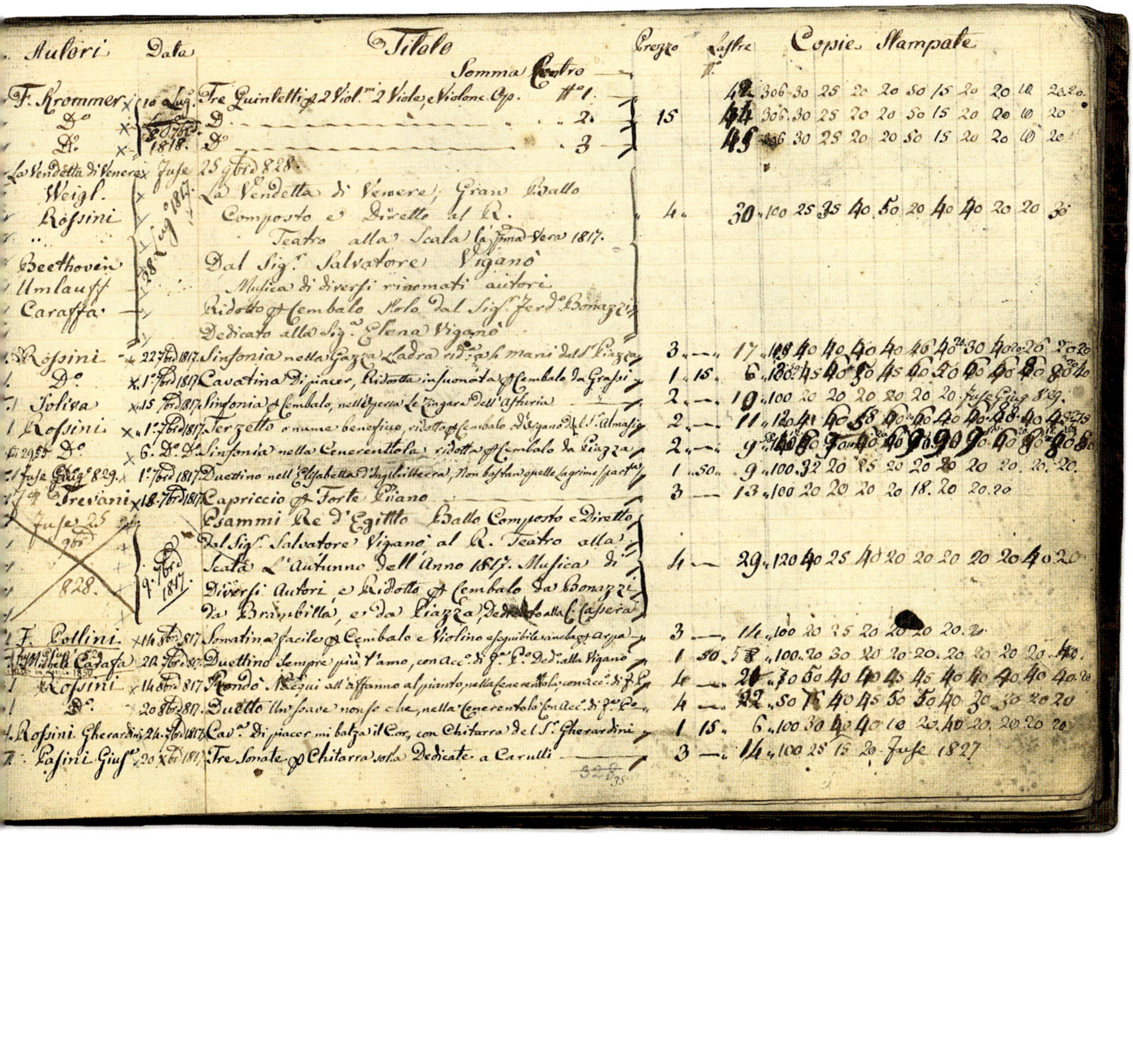

Autori	Data	Titolo	Prezzo	Lastre N.°	Copie Stampate
		Somma Contro			
F. Krommer	10 Lug.° 1818	Tre Quintetti p. 2 Viol.ni 2 Viole, e Violone Op. N.° 1	15	42	306 30 25 20 20 50 15 20 20 10 20 20
D.°		D.° 2		44	306 30 25 20 20 50 15 20 20 10 20
D.°		D.° 3		45	306 30 25 20 20 50 15 20 20 10 20
La Vendetta di Venere / Weigl. / Rossini / Beethoven / Umlauff / Caraffa	fuse 25 9bre 828. / 28 lug.° 1817	La Vendetta di Venere; Gran Ballo Composto e Diretto al R. Teatro alla Scala la p.ma vera 1817. Dal Sig.r Salvatore Viganò Musica di diversi rinomati autori Ridotto p. Cembalo Solo dal Sig.r Ferd.° Bonazzi Dedicato alla Sig.a Elena Viganò	4	30	100 25 35 40 50 20 40 40 20 20 30
Rossini	22 7bre 1817	Sinfonia nella Gazza Ladra rid.a a 4 mani dal S.r Piazza	3	17	100 40 40 40 40 40 40 30 40 20 20 20 20 [partly illegible]
D.°	1.° 7bre 1817	Cavatina Di piacer, Ridotta in suonata p. Cembalo da Grassi	1 15	6	180 45 40 50 45 40 50 40 40 80 80 40 [partly illegible]
Soliva	15 7bre 1817	Sinfonia p. Cembalo, nell'opera Le Zingare dell'Asturia	2	10	100 20 20 20 20 20 20. fuse Giug. 829.
Rossini	1.° 7bre 1817	Terzetto o nume benefico, ridotto p. Cembalo d'Organo dal S.r Almasio	2	11	120 4[illegible] 40 58 40 40 40 40 88 40 45 [partly illegible]
fuse 2955 D.°	6. D.° D.°	Sinfonia nella Cenerentola, ridotta p. Cembalo da Piazza	2	9	[illegible]
fuse Giug. 829.	1.° 7bre 1817	Duettino nell'Elisabetta d'Inghilterra, Non bastan quelle lagrime p. p.te	1 50	9	100 32 20 25 20 20 20 20 20 20 20
Trevani	18 7bre 1817	Capriccio p. Forte Piano	3	13	100 20 20 20 20 18 20 20 20
fuse 25 9bre 828.	9. 7bre 1817	Psammi Re d'Egitto Ballo Composto e Diretto dal Sig.r Salvatore Viganò al R. Teatro alla Scala L'Autunno dell'Anno 1817. Musica di Diversi Autori e Ridotto p. Cembalo da Bonazzi da Brambilla, e da Piazza, Dedicato alla C. Cassera	4	29	120 40 25 40 20 20 20 20 20 40 20
F. Pollini	14 8bre 1817	Sonatina facile p. Cembalo e Violino eseguibile anche a 3 [illegible]	3	14	100 20 25 20 20 20 20 20
Michele Carafa	20 8bre 1817	Duettino Sempre più t'amo, con acc.° di F. P.e Ded.° alla Viganò	1 50	5	100 20 30 20 20 20 20 20 20 20 40
Rossini	14 8bre 1817	Rondò Segui all'affanno al pianto, nella Cenerentola, con acc.° di F. P.e	4	20	70 50 40 40 45 45 40 40 40 40 40 20
D.°	20 8bre 1817	Duetto Un soave non so che, nella Cenerentola con Acc.° di F. P.e	4	22	50 75 40 45 50 50 40 30 30 20 20
Rossini. Gherardini	24 8bre 1817	Cav.na Di piacer mi balza il Cor, con Chitarra del S.r Gherardini	1 15	6	100 30 40 40 10 20 40 20 20 20 20
Pasini Giuse.	20 Xbre 1817	Tre Sonate p. Chitarra sola Dedicate a Carulli	3	14	100 25 15 20. fuse 1827
		328			

Salomea Kruscenis protagonista del « Madama Butterfly entusiasticamente a plaudita al Gran di Brescia nel 19(nella più famosa cita data in ques illustre teatro di t dizione, caro a Ve di, Mascagni, Puc ni, Boito e ad inte preti come Tamag e Beniamino Gi Puccini non dimen cò mai i fischi ed clamori di Milano non volle più c l'opera fosse rapp sentata alla Sca Butterfly sarebbe t nata alla Scala do la morte del ma stro, quando già veva fatto piange di commozione pubblico di tutti maggiori teatri eu pei ed americani.

MORTE E RESURREZIONE DI MADAMA BUTTERFLY

Indegnamente giustiziata alla Scala nel febbraio 1904, l'opera di Puccini ottenne a Brescia la sua rivincita pochi mesi dopo.

Se avverrà che qualcuno dedichi al Teat Grande di Brescia una monografia diligente affettuosa, certo non mancherà di inserire u pagina d'onore per la meritata sorte ch'esso eb di riconsacrare e affidare alla storia una de più popolari ed amate opere di Giacomo Pu cini: Madama Butterfly, *che il pubblico del Scala aveva indegnamente giustiziato la sera d 17 febbraio 1904. Molto si è detto e scritto p cercare di spiegare l'esito catastrofico di qu*

22

192—Review of *Madama Butterfly* by Giacomo Puccini

sta opera, travolta da una delle peggiori burrasche che la storia del teatro lirico ricordi. Claudio Sartori, uno fra i più autorevoli musicologhi nostri, in un suo libro recente, pervaso da una critica forse troppo acerba e severa, attribuisce l'insuccesso ad un errore di sensibilità del Maestro. « Puccini — egli scrive — si presentava dopo tanto tempo, glorioso della sua fama internazionale, invidiato per la sua fortuna, e non rispettato per la sua ben nota acidità verso i colleghi coetanei, illudendosi di presenziare a una cerimonia di collaudo della sua gloria. E fu invece chiamato davanti ad un severo tribunale, con giudici forse anche mal disposti. Si presentò con un'opera che sin dalle prime battute riecheggiava un tema della Bohème, e fu proprio questo particolare che scatenò le prime ire del pubblico. E se l'opera non era « un'opera diabetica e automobilisticamente infortunata », come fu malevolmente chiamata, (la compose soffrendo di diabete e immobilizzato da un sinistro automobilistico) è certo però che gli avvenimenti spiacevoli che afflissero nel periodo di preparazione il musicista, se non influirono sulla partitura tolsero però all'autore quel senso critico così acuto che fino allora l'avevano sostenuto. Sarebbe bastata — scrive sempre il Sartori — una attenta rimeditazione dell'opera prima di presentarla al pubblico per evitare il disastro. Ma Giulio Ricordi era vecchio e stanco, i librettisti (che erano, come è noto, Giacosa e Illica) avevano da tempo rinunciato alle faticose discussioni, direttore era Cleofonte Campanini e con Toscanini nessuno s'era consigliato ».

Ed infatti Toscanini fu l'unico che paventò l'insuccesso. Eppure, giunti alla fatale sera, sembrava che tutti corressero ad un trionfo, e vi si preparassero con temeraria baldanza. Giacosa s'era fatto segnare una poltrona di prima fila per godere meglio del successo. Rosina Storchio, che fu la prima mirabile interprete dell'opera, ha dettato ad un giornalista una cronaca, rimasta inedita, della tumultuosa e babelica serata. L'abbiamo trovata nelle sue carte e fra i suoi ricordi, con tracce di lagrime. « Puccini — scrisse la celebre cantante — venne a picchiare al mio camerino che scoccavano le nove, dicendomi: « Rosina, ci siamo... » Campanini era già sceso in orchestra. Mi accosto al velario. La Scala rigurgitava da aver paura. Mi ritiro verso le quinte e sento l'attacco vivacissimo dell'inizio. Con la sinistra mi premo il cuore mentre con la destra mi faccio il segno della Croce. Puccini, che mi vede, s'apparta per segnarsi anche lui di nascosto. Gli episodi, troppi, che si succedono nella prima parte dell'atto, finiscono per stancare il pubblico.

Un comprimario, rientrato fra le quinte, mormora spaventato: « Buon Dio! Che pubblico! Non fa che tossire! Maledetto! » Io sudo freddo. Dalle prime frasi che canto avverto dal pubblico

Il gruppo degli interpreti della prima rappresentazione di « Madama Butterfly » al teatro Grande di Brescia. Ecco i loro nomi degni di vivere nel ricordo, per il prezioso contributo dato alla risurrezione di un'eroina teatrale che rischiò di restare nel limbo della gloria a cui invece il pubblico bresciano decretò il primo trionfo. Da sinistra: Virgilio Bellati, Tisci Rubini, Luigi Bolpagni, Salomea Krusceniski, Giovanni Zanotello, il M.° Cleofonte Campanini, Galletti Gianoli, Emma Decima, Anselmo Ferrari, Gaetano Pini Corsi.

Periodicals

The archive has a number of issues of periodicals published by Ricordi over the years: there are the complete annual editions of the *Gazzetta Musicale di Milano* (1842–1902), of some years additional copies bound with a different cover that were apparently meant for internal use, and some unbound issues.

A number of issues of *Musica e Musicisti* (1902–1905) are available from 1902, in the small format, and some in the later larger format. The complete set of editions of the magazine *Ars et Labor* (1906–1912) is archived, all in bound annual volumes, plus some individual issues. *Musica d'Oggi* is available between 1919–1942 and 1958–1965.

Only the 1956 issues of *Ricordiana*, published from 1951–1957, are preserved in the archive. There is also *Rivista Minima*, edited from 1871 to 1878 by Ghislanzoni. One issue of the *Biblioteca Illustrata della Gazzetta Musicale di Milano* (No. 3/1888) is available, containing some illustrated stories by Alfredo Montalti. The first edition of July 10, 1864 and the volume of the year 1865 of the *Giornale della Società del Quartetto* are available. Bound annual volumes (for 1847 and from 1850 to 1859) of the magazine *Italia Musicale*, published by Lucca, are archived.

193—Cover of the *Biblioteca Illustrata della Gazzetta Musicale di Milano*, supplement to the music periodical published by Casa Ricordi, 1888

ANNO 63 Vol. II.
15 AGOSTO 1908
ARS & LABOR
· MVSICA & MVSICISTI ·
RIVISTA MENSILE ILLVSTRATA
DIRETTORE: GIVLIO RICORDI
CENT. 50 ESTERO 75
G. RICORDI & C.
– EDITORI –

194—*Ars et Labor*, artwork by Marcello Dudovich, 1908

195—*Musica e Musicisti*, artwork by Leopoldo Metlicovitz, 1903

196—Cover of *Musica d'Oggi*, 1920

197—Cover of *Ricordiana*, 1951

Index of Names

A

Adami, Giuseppe (1878–1946), playwright and librettist
Alfano, Franco (1876–1954), composer
Arosio, Giuseppina, wife of Tito I Ricordi

B

Babini, Gianni, head of the Ricordi publishing house from 1982
Battaglia, Giacinto, journalist, publisher ofthe *Gazzetta Musicale di Milano*
Battistelli, Giorgio (*1953), composer
Battisti, Lucio (1943–1998), cantautore
Belasco, David (1853–1931), playwright
Bellini, Vincenzo (1801–1835), composer
Benelli, Sem (1877–1949), poet, dramatist and librettist
Benvenuti, Giacomo (1885–1943), composer and musicologist
Berg, Alban (1885–1935), composer
Berio, Luciano (1925–2003), composer
Bernstein, Leonard (1918–1990), composer
Boito, Arrigo (1842–1918), librettist and composer
Bozzotti, Erminio, shareholder of Ricordi KG from 1888
Brassens, Georges (1921–1981), chansonnier
Brel, Jacques (1929–1978), chansonnier
Brivio, Giuditta, wife of Giulio Ricordi
Broussard, Fausto (1927–2002), editor-in-chief at Ricordi 1960–1996
Brüggemann, Alfred (1873–1944), music journalist and translator
Burgmein, Jules, pseudonym of Giulio Ricordi
Bussotti, Sylvano (*1931), composer
Buzzati, Dino (1906–1972), writer

C

Callas, Maria (1923–1977), opera singer
Carey, Mariah (*1970), pop singer
Casella, Alfredo (1883–1947), composer
Castelnuovo-Tedesco, Mario (1895–1968), composer
Catalani, Alfredo (1854–1893), composer
Cesari, Gaetano (1870–1934), musicologist and librarian
Chailly, Luciano (1920–2002), composer
Cherubini, Luigi (1760–1842), composer
Clausetti, Carlo (1869–1943), son of Pietro Clausetti, arranger and composer, headed the Casa Ricordi branch in Naples from 1919–1940 together with Renzo Valcarenghi, managing director of Casa Ricordi.
Clausetti, Eugenio, son of Carlo Clausetti
Clausetti, Margherita, wife of Carlo Clausetti
Clausetti, Pietro (1817–1892), son of Carlo Clausetti, publisher, head of the Naples branch from 1870 to 1892.
Clausetti, Pietro (1904–1963), son of Carlo Clausetti and Margherita Cosselli-Kuh, composer and conductor
Colombo, Alfredo, managing director of Ricordi from 1952
Colombo, Franco, music journalist, son of Alfredo Colombo
Corghi, Azio (*1937), composer

D

D'Annunzio, Gabriele (1863–1938), writer
Donatoni, Franco (1927–2000), composer
Donizetti, Gaetano (1797–1848), composer
Dotto, Gabriele (*1952), musicologist, editor at Ricordi 1979–1986, then editorial director as well as head of the Archivio Storico 1992–2001
Dudovich, Marcello (1878–1962), painter and poster designer

E

Edel, Alfredo (1856–1912), painter and illustrator
Eötvös, Peter (*1944), composer and conductor
Erba, Luigi, shareholder of Ricordi KG from 1888

F

Ferneyhough, Brian (*1943), composer
Festa, Felice, copper engraver and music supplies dealer
Filippi, Filippo (1830–1887), music critic, publisher of the *Gazzetta Musicale di Milano*
Finzi, Aldo (1891–1944), composer
Francesconi, Luca (*1956), composer
Franchetti, Alberto (1860–1942), composer
Freud, Sigmund (1856–1939), founder of psychoanalysis

G

Gaber, Giorgio (1939–2003), cantautore
Gabrieli, Andrea (1510–1586), composer
Gabrieli, Giovanni (1557–1613), composer
Gervasoni, Stefano (*1962), composer
Gesualdo di Venosa, Carlo (~1560–1613), composer
Ghislanzoni, Antonio (1824–1893), librettist, publisher of the *Rivista Minima*
Giacompol, Giuseppe, head of the São Paulo branch from 1927
Giordano, Umberto (1867–1948), composer
Gnecchi, Francesco, shareholder of Ricordi KG from 1888
Goebbels, Heiner (*1952), composer
Gossett, Philip (*1941), musicologist
Gramsci, Antonio (1891–1937), politician and philosopher
Grisey, Gérard (1946–1998), composer
Guastoni, Mimma (*1941), employee of Ricordi from the 1960s; manager from 1981, then managing director 1995–1998

H

Hauptmann, Gerhart (1862–1946), writer
Henneberg, Claus–Hobe (1936–1998), librettist and stage director
Henze, Hans Werner (1926–2012), composer
Hohenstein, Adolf (1854–1928), painter, illustrator and set designer
Huber, Klaus (*1924), composer
Humperdinck, Engelbert (1854–1921), composer

J

Jannacci, Enzo (*1935), cantautore
John, Elton (*1947), pop singer
Jouhaud, Stefano, music supplies trader in Florence

K

Keats, John (1795–1821), poet
Korngold, Erich Wolfgang (1897–1957), composer

L

Lagerlöf, Selma (1858–1940), writer
Leoncavallo, Ruggero (1857–1919), composer
Lindberg, Magnus (*1858), composer
Liszt, Franz (1811–1886), composer
Lombardi, Luca (*1945), composer
Lucca, Francesco (1802–1872), publisher

M

Maderna, Bruno (1920–1973), composer
Mainardi, Matteo, musicologist
Malipiero, Gian Francesco (1882–1973), composer
Manzoni, Alessandro (1785–1873), writer
Manzoni, Giacomo (*1932), composer
Marinetti, Filippo Tommaso (1876–1944), writer, originator of "Futurism" (1909)
Mascagni, Pietro (1863–1945), composer
Mataloni, Jenner (1898–1968), director of La Scala 1932–1942
Mayr, Simone (1763–1845), composer
Mazzucato, Alberto (1813–1877), music teacher and conductor, publisher of the *Gazzetta Musicale di Milano*
Menotti, Gian Carlo (1911–2007), singer
Mercadante, Giuseppe Saverio (1795–1870), composer
Metlicovitz, Leopoldo (1868–1944), painter and graphic designer
Monroe, Marilyn (1926–1962), actress
Montemezzi, Italo (1875–1952), composer
Monteverdi, Claudio (1567–1643), composer

N

Nava, Antonio (~1755–1826), guitarist, singer, composer
Neuwirth, Olga (*1968), composer
Nicolodi, Fiamma, musicologist
Nieder, Fabio (*1957), composer
Nono, Luigi (1924–1990), composer

O

Origoni, Carlo, head of the Ricordi publishingcompany from 1976

P

Pagh–Paan, Younghi (*1945), composer
Palanti, Giuseppe (1881–1946), painter and set designer
Pannain, Guido (1891–1977), musicologist and composer
Paoli, Gino (*1934), cantautore
Persico, Mario (1892–1977), composer
Pestalozza, Luciana (1929–2012), editorial director at Ricordi 1964–1992, co-founder of the "Musica nel nostro tempo" concert series
Petrassi, Goffredo (1904–2003), composer
Pick-Mangiagalli, Riccardo (1882–1949), pianist and composer
Pirandello, Luigi (1867–1936), writer and playwright
Pisa, Giuseppe, shareholder of Ricordi KG from 1888
Pizzetti, Ildebrando (1880–1968), composer
Pollini, Francesco (1762–1846), pianist and composer
Puccini, Giacomo (1858–1924), composer

R

Rapetti, Mariano (1911–1982), pianist and lyricist, head of Radio Record Ricordi
Rapetti Mogol, Giulio, known as Mogol (*1936), lyricist
Respighi, Ottorino (1879–1936), composer
Ricordi, Camillo (1908–1954), son of Manolo Ricordi
Ricordi, Carlo Emanuele (Nanni) (1932–2012), founder and director of Dischi Ricordi
Ricordi, Claudio (*1944), great-grandson of Giulio's brother Giuseppe
Ricordi, Emanuele (Manolo) (1876–1940), son of Giulio Ricordi, head of Officine Ricordi
Ricordi, Giovanni (1785–1853), founder of the publishing company
Ricordi, Giulio (1840–1912), son of Tito I Ricordi, head of the publishing company from 1888–1912
Ricordi, Marisa, wife of Nanni Ricordi
Ricordi, Tito I (1811–1888), son of Giovanni Ricordi, head of the publishing company from 1853–1888
Ricordi, Tito II (1865–1933), son of Giulio, head of the publishing company from 1912–1919
Riehm, Rolf (*1937), composer
Rignano, Guido (*1924), managing director of Casa Ricordi 1964–1994
Richie, Lionel (*1949), pop singer
Rossato, Arturo (1882–1942), journalist and playwright
Rossini, Gioacchino (1792–1868), composer

S

Sachs, Harvey (*1946), music journalist, biographer of Arturo Toscanini
Sanguineti, Edoardo (1930–2010), writer
Sartori, Claudio (1913–1994), musicologist
Scarlatti, Domenico (1685–1757), composer
Schönberg, Arnold (1874–1951), composer, originator of "twelve-tone music"
Sciarrino, Salvatore (*1947), composer
Shelley, Percy Bysshe (1792–1822), poet
Sonzogno, Edoardo (1836–1920), publisher
Starace, Achille (1889–1945), secretary of the Fascist Party
Steinecke, Wolfgang († 1961), head of the Cultural Office in Darmstadt
Strauss, Richard (1864–1949), composer
Strazza, Gustavo, shareholder of Ricordi KG from 1888
Svevo, Italo (Hector Aron Schmitz) (1861–1928), writer

T

Tenaglia, Raffaele (1884–1975), director of the rental archives and editor-in-chief at Ricordi, 1913–1961
Tenco, Luigi (1938–1967), cantautore
Toscanini, Arturo (1867–1957), conductor
Tosti, Francesco Paolo (1846–1916), singer and composer

V

Vaccaj, Nicola (1790–1848), composer and music teacher
Valcarenghi, Renzo (1860–1947), managing director of Casa Ricordi 1919–1943
Valcarenghi, Guido, son of Renzo, head of the Buenos Aires branch from 1924, managing director of the company from 1952
Vanoni, Ornella (*1934), singer
Verdi, Giuseppe (1813–1901), composer
Visconti, Luchino (1906–1976), movie director
Vittadini, Franco (1884–1948), composer
Vivaldi, Antonio (1678–1741), composer

W

Wagner, Richard (1813–1883), composer
Webern, Anton (1883–1945), composer
Wolf-Ferrari, Ermanno (1876–1948), composer

Z

Zandonai, Riccardo (1883–1944), composer
Zedda, Alberto (*1928), conductor and musicologist

Bibliography

A

Adami, Giuseppe: *Giulio Ricordi*, Milan 1945

Amodeo, Immacolata: *Das Opernhafte. Eine Studie zum "gusto melodrammatico" in Italien und Europa*, Bielefeld 2007.

B

Baia Curioni, Stefano: *Mercanti dell'opera. Storie di Casa Ricordi*, Milan 2011.

Berengo, Marino: *Intellettuali e librai nella Milano della Restaurazione*. Milan 1980.

C

Carapella, Eleonora: *"Musicisti ebrei nell'Italia delle persecuzioni: il caso Aldo Finzi"*. www.aldo-finzi.com

Carner, Mosco: *Puccini*, Frankfurt a. M., 1996.

Castelnuovo-Tedesco, Mario: *Una vita di musica (un libro di ricordi). Catalogo delle opere. A cura di James Westby. Introduzione di Mila de Santis. Cura editoriale di Ulla Casalini*, Fiesole 2005.

Celeste Aida. Percorso storico musicale tra passato e futuro, Milan 2006.

G

Giuseppe Verdi, Giulio Ricordi: corrispondenza e immagini 1881–1890, a cura di Franca Cella e Pierluigi Petrobelli, Milan 1982

Goethe, Johann Wolfgang: *Italienische Reise*, Frankfurt am Main 1976.

Grafica Ricordi, dal manifesto storico alla produzione d'avanguardia, a cura di Giovanni Sangiorgi, Giorgio Mascherpa, Giulia Veronesi, Rome 1967.

I

Il Risorgimento Grafico, raccolta mensile di saggi grafici e scritti tecnici diretta da Raffaello Bertieri. Fascicolo dedicato al centenario della Ditta Ricordi & C. di Milano, Milan 1908.

J

Jensen, Luke: *Giuseppe Verdi & Giovanni Ricordi. With notes on Francesco Lucca. From Oberto to La traviata*, New York and London 1989.

L

Libretti d'opera italiani dal Seicento al Novecento, a cura di Giovanna Gronda und Paolo Fabbri, Milan 1997.

M

Mainardi, Matteo: *"Musica, Fascismo, editoria. Casa Ricordi ta rinnovamento e tradizione", in: Editori e lettori. La produzione libraria in Italia nella prima metà del Novecento. A cura di Luisa Finocchi e Ada Gigli Marchetti*, Milan 2000, pp. 99–116.

Milano, laboratorio musicale del Novecento – Scritti in onore di Luciana Pestalozza, ed. by Oreste Bossini, Milan 2009.

Musica, musicisti, editoria: 175 anni di Casa Ricordi, Milan 1983.

N

Nicolodi, Fiamma: *Gusti e tendenze del novecento musicale in Italia. Prefazione di Fedele d'Amico*, Florence 1982.

P

Pauls, Birgit: *Giuseppe Verdi und das Risorgimento. Ein politischer Mythos im Prozeß der Nationenbildung*, Berlin 1996.

Q

Quaderni dell'I.R.TE.M., 14, Roma 1993: *Serie 5: Cronologie. N. 1: Le otto stagioni di Toscanini alla Scala 1921–1929, di Carlo Marinelli Roscioni.*

S

Sachs, Harvey: *Toscanini. Eine Biographie, übers. von Hans-Horst Henschen*, Munich 1980.

Sartori, Claudio: *Casa Ricordi 1808/1958. Profilo storico. Itinerario grafico editoriale*, Milan 1958.

T

That's Opera: 200 years of Italian Music, Munich/Berlin/London/New York 2008.

Ti ricordi Nanni? Con Nanni Ricordi, l'uomo che inventò i cantautori, Milan 2010.

Trezzini, Lamberto/Curtolo, Angelo: *Oltre le quinte. Idee, cultura e organizzazione del teatro musicale in Italia*, Venice 1983.

V

Vergani, Orio: *I Ricordi: immagine di un'epoca*, Milan 1994 (extended new edition of *Piccolo viaggio in un archivio*, Milan 1953)

W

Winkler, Heinrich August: *Geschichte des Westens. Von den Anfängen in der Antike bis zum 20. Jahrhundert*, Munich 2009.

The quotes on pp. 6, 77, 101, 131, 143 are taken from *Archivio Storico Ricordi. Un progetto per il terzo millennio*, Milan 2001.

Image Credits

Cover

Raragramma by Sylvano Bussotti,
autograph score, 1982

2

9—photograph by Pagliano e Ricordi

4

20—photograph by Emilio Sommariva

5

34—photograph by Publifoto
35—photograph by Publifoto
36—photograph by Publifoto

6

39—photograph by Bovio
41—photograph by Roto

7

42—photograph by De Narde
43—photograph by Roto
45—photograph by Carlo Cisventi
54—photograph by Galliano Passerini
56—photograph by Giuseppe Molteni
58—photograph by Mimmo Chianura/AGF
59—photograph by Guy Vivien

9

106—photograph by Pietro Paolo Bertieri
111—photograph by Kossak
112—photograph by White
113—photograph by Byron

10

118—photograph by Greguoli

11

122—photograph by Manfredi Bellati
124—photograph by Graziano Arici
125—photograph by Guido Wilhelm

12

129—photograph by Publifoto
138—photograph by Sara Scanderebech

Overview

175—photograph by White
176—photograph by Giacomo Brogi
177—photograph by Giulio Rossi

Imprint

Project Management "Archivio Storico Ricordi"
Pierluigi Ledda
Helen Müller

Author (manuscript)
Caroline Lüderssen

Scientific Consultation
Gabriele Dotto

Image Research
Maria Pia Ferraris

Photo Editing
Chiara Gasparini
Valeria Luti

Project Coordination
Alissa Nordmeier

Translation
Lara Wagner

Layout
Stan Hema GmbH
www.stanhema.com

Printing
Mohn Media Mohndruck GmbH

Please direct all requests on images
and archival contents to:
Archivio Storico Ricordi
c/o Biblioteca Braidense
Via Brera 28
20121 Milan, Italy

archivio@archivioricordi.com
www.archivioricordi.com

Distributed in the trade by Prestel Verlag
A member of Verlagsgruppe Random House GmbH
Neumarkter Strasse 28 · 81673 Munich

978-3-7913-5623-5
www.prestel.com